Sushi
Cookbook
FOR BEGINNERS

Sushi Cookbook

FOR BEGINNERS

100 Step-by-Step Recipes to Make Sushi at Home

CHIKA RAVITCH

Photography Antonis Achilleos

ROCKRIDGE
PRESS

Interior and Cover Designer: Lisa Schreiber
Art Producer: Janice Ackerman
Editor: Marjorie DeWitt
Production Editor: Andrew Yackira

Custom Photography: © 2020 Antonis Achilleos. Food Styling by Gordon Sawyer.

Illustration Courtesy of iStock: p. x, 14, 24, 66, 124, 142
Photography Courtesy of iStock: p. 40, 49, 52; p. 165: © Kate Lewis
Illustration Courtesy of Shutterstock: p. vi, viii, 27, 28, 32, 33, 38, 50, 55, 70, 83, 87, 95, 99, 106, 107, 109, 115, 117, 118, 119, 120, 129, 135, 139, 146, 148, 149, 150, 151, 152, 153, 154, 155, 156, 157, 158, 159, 160, 161, 162, 163

ISBN: Print 978-1-64611-878-6 | eBook 978-1-64611-879-3

R0

To my mother (March 10, 1947–April 25, 1995) for giving me limitless love. To my husband, Frank, for depthless support in every way.

Contents

Introduction

Sushi is no longer just a Japanese food—it's now all the rage around the world. Many sushi dishes are pieces of art and beautifully created based on multicultural tastes. This creativity and the unconventional idea behind sushi ultimately increased its popularity and impressed me when I first ate it.

Traditional Japanese sushi is prepared by sushi chefs. In Japan they are technically called craftspeople, and not chefs, and the sushi they prepare is considered an important craft. The reason this terminology is used is that it generally takes three to five years to become a sushi chef, and doing so requires special techniques and a lot of patience to uphold the old traditions. Chefs in training are not able to learn how to prepare sushi in the first year, but rather they learn how to clean a restaurant, deliver, cook rice, and serve customers. After the first year they begin learning to prepare sushi in earnest. A skillful sushi chef can grab exactly the same weight and the same number of rice grains without looking each time they make nigiri sushi, and the rice isn't crushed but holds its shape completely. It's this perfection and craftsmanship that drives Japanese people to go out to restaurants rather than prepare sushi at home.

Of course, high-quality sushi is delicious, but it can be very expensive. Therefore, lately, there are many people who try to make their own sushi, even in Japan. Homemade sushi should be delicious, easy to make, and beautiful. There are many global, nontraditional, awe-inspiring sushi recipes for people to make at home.

When I was a child, my mother and my grandmother often made traditional sushi rolls and inari sushi, a popular Japanese rice ball. It was the best sushi I have had in my life. Although the fillings are the same as traditional recipes, the seasoned rice tasted different. This is one of the advantages of homemade sushi—adjusting the seasoning according to personal taste and adding any ingredients as fillings. I learned a lot about cooking from my mother and grandmother that helped me appreciate the simplicity behind making sushi. I am here to tell you how, and that making sushi is not complicated. You can do it, too.

In this book I made the recipes easy and used ingredients that are simple to find and available in the United States. There are seafood, meat, vegetarian, and vegan sushi dishes. An added benefit is that most sushi is gluten-free if you use gluten-free soy sauce. This book also includes many tips to help you make good-looking sushi. You may need a bit of practice, but with this cookbook you will easily be able to make your own sushi. Just follow the recipes and you can eat your favorite sushi anytime you want without going out to a sushi restaurant!

1

Starting Your Sushi Journey

MAKING HOMEMADE SUSHI IS NOT DIFFICULT AT ALL, AND this book is your Sushi 101 guide. It contains all the basic things you need to know about sushi, how to prepare it, necessary equipment, ingredients, etiquette, the art of serving, and useful tips. This book will fully prepare you to create sushi with confidence and fun!

The History of Sushi

About 1,300 years ago, people fermented fresh fish with salt and rice to preserve it. This was the beginning of sushi. However, the rice was used as a fermentation ingredient, and only the fish was eaten. Even today this approach is reflected in a famous regional sushi cuisine from Shiga prefecture, called *funazushi*.

Sushi, as we know it today—nigiri sushi and sushi rolls—began about 400 years ago during the Edo era. At that time there were fancy sushi restaurants and sushi stands. Busy people ate the sushi from the stand like fast food. The difference between current nigiri and Edo-era nigiri is the size. Edo-era nigiri was 1.5 times bigger than current nigiri, which is bite size.

Although sushi was a very popular food, sushi restaurants were closed by food regulators after World War II due to a shortage of food. To get around this, some restaurants made changes to their approach and required their customers to bring their own rice, which was then paired with the restaurant's sushi. As Japan experienced increased economic growth and prosperity, food regulation policies again

Glossary

There is an assortment of terms used within this book. Please familiarize yourself with these terms in order to best prepare for sushi making.

Sashimi: fresh, raw fish cut into thin slices and served with soy sauce. Most Japanese eat sashimi in a sushi restaurant as an appetizer.

Sushi: meaning "sour rice," this dish is served with rice, fish, egg, or vegetables. There are a few exceptions to this definition; for example, *soba-zushi* rolls use cooked soba instead of rice, and pickled mackerel, called *kizushi*, is eaten without rice.

Nigiri: seafood, vegetables, or egg on a flat-football-shaped bed of vinegared rice. In Japan we usually get this at a restaurant or order it for delivery so we can eat nigiri made by a well-trained sushi chef.

Maki: a sushi roll made of vinegared rice, seafood, and vegetables that is wrapped in dried seaweed, called nori, and created using a sushi-rolling mat called a *makisu*.

Futomaki: a thick, fat sushi roll using a whole (7-by-8-inch) nori sheet. Popular in western Japan.

changed and sushi service was allowed in restaurants. The year 1958 was pivotal for the sushi industry: It was the first year customers could go to a sushi bar and purchase prepared sushi from a conveyor belt. These days, fancy sushi restaurants are still frequented; however, it's sushi bars that are most popular.

The first sushi restaurant in the United States was opened in San Francisco in 1887 by a Japanese immigrant. However, all sushi restaurants owned by Japanese people were closed during World War II because of the internment of Japanese Americans. After the war, the restaurants were slowly reopened, and from the 1970s on, the sushi boom gradually expanded. Along with the popularization of sushi restaurants in the United States, many nontraditional sushi recipes were created by US-based Japanese sushi chefs to adjust to the availability of ingredients and to accommodate American tastes. For example, *uramaki*, a sushi roll with the rice on the outside, was created for Americans because many Americans didn't like the feel of eating nori, edible seaweed.

Hosomaki: a thin sushi roll using a half (7-by-4-inch) nori sheet. Popular in eastern Japan.

Uramaki: an inside-out roll with the rice on the outside.

Chirashi: a bowl of rice, seafood, vegetables, and egg.

Temari: flat, golf-ball-size portions of rice topped with seafood, vegetables, egg, and meats. Temari was recently invented and popularized because it doesn't require any special skills or equipment.

Gunkanmaki: nigiri sushi rice wrapped in nori with space at the top to hold seafood or vegetables.

Temaki: a hand-rolled cone of sushi that includes rice and fillings.

Inari sushi: a sushi rice ball simmered in sweet-savory fried bean curd.

Wasabi: a Japanese horseradish used for both sashimi and sushi dishes that has antibacterial effects and reduces the risk of food poisoning.

Gari: a Japanese pickled ginger used for sushi dishes that has antibacterial effects and also has the role of a palate freshener.

Tsuma: an important vegetable garnish for sashimi dishes that has exactly the same role as pickled ginger for sushi dishes but is used only for sashimi dishes.

The Equipment

Beginners don't need much equipment, but there are a few tools that are helpful. Below are my recommendations of must-haves and nice-to-haves to help you prioritize. Throughout the book, I'll discuss helpful substitutes, but should you choose to purchase the actual tool, you can find it at your local kitchen store, Amazon, or many Asian markets.

MUST-HAVES

MAKISU (SUSHI-ROLLING MAT) – A sushi-rolling mat is a key tool to have for creating visually stunning sushi. These mats come in bamboo, silicone, or plastic. I recommend a bamboo mat due to its flexibility, which makes it much easier to roll 7-to-8-inch-long sushi rolls evenly. Bamboo is also highly sanitary because it has antibacterial effects and eliminates odors. But it needs great care. It is essential to boil the mat to get rid of any debris and the bamboo smell before the first use. Wipe immediately with a clean, wet kitchen towel any time you see rice or other sushi ingredients stuck between the bamboo rods because it is hard to wash after the debris dries (you can avoid this problem by placing a piece of parchment paper or some plastic wrap on the bamboo mat). Handwash your makisu with water (it is not recommended to use dish soap) and dry really well in a shady area without direct sunlight. I am not as much of a fan of the silicone or plastic mats. They are not as easy for rolling because silicone mats are too flexible and the plastic mats are too hard.

SHAMOJI (RICE PADDLE) – I highly recommend purchasing a self-standing, plastic rice paddle with a nonstick gritty surface because it has the best shape for mixing and scooping rice. This type of paddle is easy to use and helps keep the kitchen clean. It's also the only tool for which I can't find any substitutes. There are wooden rice paddles, but the rice sticks too easily, which is very stressful, and they can't go in the dishwasher.

NICE TO HAVE

RICE COOKER – This is a handy tool to have but not required because I'll teach you how to cook rice in a pan. If you have a rice cooker, it makes things easier and more efficient.

CUTTING BOARDS – Sushi making requires frequent cutting. For safety, it's best to use different boards for raw fish, vegetables, cooked food, and meats. I recommend wooden cutting boards for general use with vegetables and cooked food and dishwasher-safe boards for seafood and meats. I recommend wooden boards because they are knife-friendly. They also are easy on your hand because the material absorbs the cutting vibration. When you use boards made from hard materials, like glass, for long periods of time, you subject your hand to direct vibrations every single time you cut through to the board with the knife, and this makes your hand very tired. The key with a wooden board is to wash frequently and sanitize with boiling water about once a week and every time after cutting seafood or meat.

SUSHI-OKE, HANGIRI, OR HANDAI (RICE-MIXING TUB) – This is a shallow tub made of wood that is used to mix steamed rice and sushi vinegar. It has a great shape for cooling sushi rice down, and it looks nice at a party or in pictures. Please keep in mind that this tool is a little difficult to handle. You can definitely substitute a large bowl or a high-rimmed baking sheet for this.

THE KNIFE

There are so many kinds of knives in the world, which is confusing when trying to choose which to buy. If there is a cutler near you, you can ask them for a recommendation. Be sure to hold the knives in your hand to check their heaviness and comfort before making a selection. If there is no cutler near you, don't worry; I will explain how to choose a good knife for making sushi.

How to Choose the Right Knife

For slicing seafood and cutting sushi rolls smoothly, you need a sharp knife that slices while pulling the knife toward you in one cut. A blunt knife crushes the ingredients as you slice. If you want to buy a good knife for making sushi, look for a *yanagiba* knife or a sashimi knife, which has a long, narrow blade. There are three kinds of blade materials for these knives: carbon steel, stainless steel, and ceramic. Carbon steel is the material in traditional Japanese knives and is the sharpest, but it does rust easily. Stainless steel and ceramic knives are easy to handle, but they are not as sharp as carbon steel. Yanagiba knives mostly have a single blade, so if you are left-handed, you should look for a double-bevel variety or ask to try it before buying. It is better to choose a blade that is 8 to 10 inches long and shorter than your cutting board. I like using a stainless steel yanagiba knife for cutting sashimi because it cuts smoothly, is easy to handle, and usually doesn't rust. Please remember these knives

Sharpening Your Knife

If you have or buy a knife sharpener, be sure to check what materials the sharpener can be used for (carbon, stainless steel, ceramic) and whether it is for single-bevel knives, double-bevel knives, or both, depending on your knives. A more traditional way to sharpen carbon steel or stainless steel sushi knives is to use a whetstone once a month. A sharp knife leads to less stress during food preparation. Whetstones often are numbered from #300 through #8000. The lower-number whetstones sharpen the edge really well and are used when the edge is clipped off. For sharpening a knife at home, it is better to use a whetstone between #800 and #2000. For a quick fix, when I need to sharpen my knife right here and right now, I sharpen it with the back of an earthenware plate or cup. It works temporarily. But keep in mind this is not a professional way, provides no guarantee the knife will be properly sharpened, and does not provide knife safety. Of course, perhaps the easiest way to sharpen your knives is to go to a professional knife sharpener.

are for cutting fresh fish, so do not use them to cut frozen fish, fish bones, or other hard ingredients. The edge of the knife can be easily broken. You can also shop for Japanese knives at online stores, such as Best Japanese Knives (Japanny.com) and Japanese Chefs Knife (japanesechefsknife.com). These sites have a great selection of products.

Fresh Ingredients

One of the reasons why sushi is healthy is that it contains fresh fish and vegetables. Here I list the essential fresh ingredients for sushi, and I teach you how to choose seafood that is in good condition.

SEAFOOD

TUNA (*MAGURO*) – Served raw in sashimi and sushi dishes. There are many kinds of tuna used for sushi, such as bluefin, bigeye, yellowfin, and albacore. You can buy any kind of tuna. Choose sashimi-grade meat that has a bright red color and an even grain. Avoid dark or discolored tuna. This means the tuna is old.

SALMON – Salmon has healthy fat, and it tastes very mild. It is a popular ingredient for making sashimi and sushi dishes. Be sure to choose sashimi-grade frozen salmon that is properly treated, because salmon can have anisakis (a parasite). If you really care about parasitic insects, choose only farm-raised salmon. Studies show that farm-raised fish may have fewer parasitic insects than wild-caught fish. This is true not only for salmon but also for other ocean fish. It is also important to check the fish visually when you cut. Choose salmon that has clear strings (connective tissue) if you can see them.

SMOKED SALMON – Smoked salmon brings great, rich flavor to your sushi dishes. Store-bought smoked salmon is ready to use and has a longer usage life than fresh salmon when stored in the refrigerator. It is definitely a handy and safe food.

SEARED BONITO (*KATSUO-NO-TATAKI*) – Bonito fillet is grilled briefly before being sliced and served with ponzu sauce.

SHRIMP (*EBI*) – When using for nigiri sushi and as a topping on *chirashi* sushi, buy medium-size, tail-on, un-deveined shrimp. Cooking sushi shrimp requires a little technique. The details and some tips can be found in the recipes in this book that use boiled shrimp.

YELLOWTAIL (*HAMACHI*) – Hamachi is a very popular fish for sashimi and nigiri in Japan. It has a light taste and tender texture. Choose translucent meat with red muscle.

SCALLOP (*HOTATE*) – Served as a sashimi dish and in nigiri sushi. It has a sweet taste and very soft texture. Try eating it with natural sea salt. The flavor is more pronounced than when eating it with soy sauce. Most store-bought sashimi-grade scallops are frozen. If you find fresh scallops, choose meaty, thick ones. Do not rinse scallops with water, because this makes them taste bland.

CRABMEAT (*KANI*) – When the meat is lump, it is great for making *gunkanmaki*. When the meat is well shaped, like crab legs, it is good for making nigiri sushi and sushi rolls. Also, canned crabmeat is very handy and delicious.

SALMON ROE (*IKURA*) – Great for gunkanmaki and sometimes to eat on its own. The roe pops in the mouth and then brings a very mild yet rich, delicious taste. You may find glass jars of salmon roe at grocery stores or online seafood shops.

NEGITORO – Minced sashimi tuna garnished with chopped scallion. It is served as a sushi roll and in gunkanmaki. It has a great, fluffy texture.

Sustainable Practices

To keep marine environments safe for all life, the sustainable seafood movement began in the 1990s. Sustainable seafood isn't just about preventing overfishing, but also applies to farming environments and fishing methods. Even if a fisher catches fish on the green list (best fish to choose), if the method of harvesting endangers the marine environment, it is not sustainable seafood. It is important to buy the right fish with a certification on the label, such as MSC (the Marine Stewardship Council), ASC (the Aquaculture Stewardship Council), SeaChoice, or Seafood Watch. Another way to choose the best fish is to follow a sustainable seafood consumer guide, which you can find online.

Picking the Right Fish

CHOOSE THE RIGHT FISHMONGER – Reviews are an important resource for choosing a fishmonger. Freshness, odor, how the fish is displayed (on ice), and the cleanliness of the shop are key to getting proper-quality fish. Ask your friends and neighbors and check online reviews. Also, there are some online seafood shops that can be useful for people who live in landlocked states.

VISUAL CHECK – When you buy a sashimi-grade fish fillet, check that the meat is shiny, smooth, tight, firm, and brightly colored. Also check around the fillet and choose one that has less deicing fluid, which you'll see as a murky, slightly thick liquid around the fish in the case or in the package. When the fillet has a lot of deicing fluid, that means it may have been thawed quickly, which makes the fish taste bland and smell bad.

PRODUCE AND OTHER FRESH ITEMS

EGG – An essential ingredient for traditional Japanese sushi dishes.

CUCUMBER – A useful ingredient for sushi rolls and a beautiful addition to gunkanmaki. Also, cut and carved cucumber in decorative shapes, such as flowers, is sometimes used as a garnish for sashimi dishes.

AVOCADO – This is an extremely popular ingredient that was not a traditional ingredient for sushi in Japan. About 50 years ago, sushi restaurants started serving avocado sushi, and now the Japanese love it very much.

LEAF LETTUCE – There is a traditional "salad sushi roll" with lettuce, canned tuna, imitation crab, mayonnaise, and sometimes sweet corn kernels with nori and sushi rice. Also, lettuce sometimes becomes a substitute for nori for hand-roll sushi (*temaki*).

CREAM CHEESE – Used for sushi rolls. It goes really well with salmon and shrimp.

IMITATION CRABMEAT – Very handy ingredient made with fish meat paste and good in many kinds of sushi dishes.

CORN – Versatile ingredient used for many kinds of sushi dishes. It is one of the popular sushi ingredients for kids in Japan.

SWEET ONION – Marinated sweet onion is used as a garnish for salmon nigiri sushi and is eaten on its own as a side dish.

ASPARAGUS – Boiled or fried asparagus is a great ingredient for sushi rolls and can also be a garnish for creative sushi rolls.

SHIITAKE MUSHROOMS AND SPINACH – Both ingredients are essentials for traditional sushi rolls. They are traditionally cooked with a sweet–savory dashi sauce.

MEATS – Sometimes meat, such as chicken, beef, bacon, or ham, is used for homemade sushi dishes. Nowadays, in fancy sushi restaurants in Japan, roast beef and roast duck nigiri sushi are very popular.

CARROT AND RADISH – Both are used as a garnish for sushi dishes. As with cucumber, cut and carved carrots and radishes in decorative shapes, such as flowers, are sometimes used as a garnish for sashimi dishes.

DAIKON RADISH – Important garnish for sashimi dishes. It has antibacterial effects and reduces the chance of contracting food poisoning. Slice into very thin strips and place sashimi on the daikon radish to serve.

***SHISO* (PERILLA/JAPANESE BASIL)** – A Japanese herb that grows naturally in Japan. It is used as a garnish for sashimi dishes. As with daikon radish, it has antibacterial effects and reduces the risk of food poisoning. Substitute basil leaf or parsley, which have microbicidal properties.

Pantry Ingredients

Here I will show you some ingredients you can stock in your pantry. There are also some handy dried and canned ingredients you can substitute for fresh ingredients. You can get most of these at Asian markets or on Amazon.

SHORT-GRAIN WHITE RICE (SUSHI RICE) – Stock in the pantry and, once it is opened, put the rice with its bag in a zip-top bag and keep it in the refrigerator.

SUSHI NORI – This type of dried seaweed usually comes in 7-by-8-inch sheets. There are two sides—one is shiny and the other is slightly rough—and traditionally, sushi rice is placed on the rough side. Once the package is opened, put the nori in a zip-top bag and keep it in the refrigerator.

SOY SAUCE – Generally people say sashimi-grade fish goes well with tamari soy sauce. There are about 10,000 kinds of soy sauce in Japan alone, so it can be good to find your favorite soy sauce for your sushi. Once it's opened, keep it in the refrigerator unless otherwise instructed.

DRIED KELP (DASHI KOMBU) – Cooking sushi rice with dried kelp adds a richer, umami flavor to the rice.

ROASTED SESAME SEEDS – Used to garnish the outside of *uramaki* sushi rolls and sometimes mixed in sushi rice.

WASABI PASTE/WASABI POWDER – For the paste type of wasabi, once it's opened, keep it in the refrigerator. For the powder type, close the lid tightly and keep it in the pantry.

PICKLED SUSHI GINGER (*GARI*) – If fresh young ginger, the central ingredient of homemade pickled sushi ginger, cannot be found, store-bought pickled ginger is very useful. Once it's opened, keep it in the refrigerator.

CANNED SEASONED FRIED BEAN CURD – This makes cooking *inari* sushi much easier, and it is definitely a time-saver.

WAKAME – Used for soup, in salad, and as a garnish for sashimi dishes. Sushi nori, wakame, and kelp are different kinds of seaweed. Wakame is thin, not gooey, easy to eat, and high in minerals.

DASHI STOCK POWDER – Used for simmering sushi vegetables and soups. Bonito dashi powder, which is the most common, is useful. If you would like vegetable stock, choose kombu dashi powder.

The Wasabi in Your Bowl

Even in Japan, we don't eat pure, grated, fresh Japanese horseradish root—real wasabi—very often. Most processed wasabi products are made with a mixture of Western horseradish and Japanese horseradish wasabi. This is because wasabi is hard to grow and takes a long time to be cultivated, so grocery stores don't stock pure wasabi regularly, and when they do, the price is high. Therefore, people tend to use processed wasabi paste or wasabi powder because it is easy and less expensive. In Japan there is a rule that when the proportion of real wasabi is 50 percent or more of the total content, the product can be displayed with "Made with real wasabi," and when the ratio is less than 50 percent, the product must be displayed as "Containing real wasabi." However, processed wasabi products also use the leaves and stems of Japanese horseradish, even though pure wasabi is basically just the grated root of Japanese horseradish. For all these reasons, if you have the chance to get a fresh wasabi root, please try it because it has an amazing, mildly spicy, fresh taste that is totally different from processed wasabi. Here, I will list some better wasabi products that you can buy on Amazon and at some Asian markets, and I will show you the pros and cons of each. But keep in mind, Western horseradish can also fill the same role as wasabi, which is to provide an antibacterial effect and reduce the risk of food poisoning, so you can choose wasabi or Western horseradish according to your preference.

- Authentic Japanese Shizuoka Wasabi Paste by Tamaruya
- S&B Premium Wasabi Paste in tube (no color added)

Pros: Made with Japanese horseradish and doesn't contain Western horseradish at all. Good taste.
Cons: Contains many preservatives.

- S&B Selected Wasabi Powder

Pros: Made with all natural ingredients and no additives.
Cons: Mixture of Western horseradish, mustard, and wasabi.

The Etiquette of Eating Sushi

There are many rules of etiquette in Japanese food culture, not only for eating sushi but also for eating other things and even at the dining table at home. Some of these rules are excessive and outdated. Things are becoming more casual as times have changed. For example, originally it was considered polite to eat nigiri sushi with your hands, but today either using chopsticks or eating by hand is considered polite. Here I list some basic rules of etiquette for eating at a sushi restaurant in Japan.

- You can eat sushi either with chopsticks or with your hands. A wet towel is served in Japanese restaurants.

- It is preferable to start with a mild, light-tasting fish and then progress to gradually fattier fish so you can enjoy tasting many kinds of seafood.

- When you eat nigiri sushi, slightly tilt the nigiri to the side and dip the edge of the fish in a small amount of soy sauce so the rice doesn't absorb much soy sauce and you can enjoy the natural, fresh taste of the seafood. Do not remove the seafood from the nigiri sushi. Rather, dip it in the soy sauce and put it back on the rice.

- Eat nigiri sushi in one bite. Do not bite through half of the nigiri.

- Dip the edge of a sushi roll in soy sauce. In Japan, sushi rolls are served with soy sauce on the side and are not drizzled with mayonnaise or spicy sauce.

- When you eat chirashi sushi, dip just the seafood in soy sauce, put it back on the rice, and then eat it all together.

- When you eat sashimi with wasabi, put a small amount of wasabi on the sashimi and dip in soy sauce. Do not dissolve the wasabi in the soy sauce.

- If you don't like wasabi, feel free to tell the sushi chef. Traditionally, sushi chefs put wasabi between rice and seafood in most nigiri sushi and in thin sushi rolls.

- Generally in a Japanese sushi restaurant, people eat sashimi as an appetizer and eat nigiri as a main dish. If you order sushi rolls and a soup after that, the chefs tend to think you have finished your meal.

The Proper Use of Pickled Ginger

Pickled ginger is always served with sushi dishes because it reduces the risk of food poisoning due to its antibacterial effect, it freshens your mouth so you can enjoy the taste of the next piece of sushi after eating sushi with fatty fish, and it warms our blood because raw fish is said to cool down our bodies. For these reasons, it is better to eat the ginger between eating each piece of sushi. In addition, pickled ginger is sometimes used for brushing sushi with soy sauce, where the ingredients are lightly dipped in soy sauce, such as for gunkanmaki. As an aside, you may see that pickled ginger has a light pink color. This is because the pickled ginger is made with young ginger harvested before maturity. This kind of ginger has a slightly pink color and tastes very mild, which makes for delicious pickled ginger. However, some store-bought sushi ginger is dyed.

The Art of Serving Sushi

In Japanese cuisine, it is said that we judge a meal using the five senses: touch, taste, vision, smell, and sound. Visual appeal is deeply connected with taste. When a dish has beautiful final presentation, people tend to feel it is tastier. This doesn't mean we have to decorate dishes excessively. Japanese sushi is generally served simply yet beautifully. The setting fully represents the true natural beauty of sushi ingredients.

- Prepare some wet towels individually for people who may eat sushi by hand.

- Sushi is always served with some pickled ginger.

- Serve any sushi that doesn't have a drizzled sauce with small, shallow plates that can be filled with soy sauce.

- It is preferable that sashimi is served with *shiso* (substitute basil leaves or parsley), thinly sliced daikon radish, or some decoratively cut and carved vegetables, such as cucumber, radish, and carrot.

- The same kind of sushi should always have equal sizes and shapes. For example, nigiri sushi should always have the same size and shape of rice. Sushi rolls should be shaped in beautiful circles or squares.

- For creative sushi rolls, garnish with some nuts, crispy fried onions, or tempura batter bits, and drizzle some sauce over the sushi rolls.

CHAPTER

2

Preparing Your Ingredients

THIS CHAPTER WILL TEACH YOU THE PRACTICAL STEPS FOR preparing sushi, such as making sushi rice, pitfalls to avoid, and how to prepare seafood, vegetables, and other items. If you find all the information overwhelming, it is helpful to remember that in practice, there are only a few basic rules you must know to prepare sushi. Once you understand these basic rules, you will have a lot of options, because sushi creation is versatile.

Rice

Traditionally, *sushi* is a name for dishes that combine vinegared rice with some fresh ingredients, such as sashimi fish and/or vegetables. To make good sushi rice, you should use short-grain white rice from Japan (sometimes called sushi rice and often available at your local supermarket) and be sure to measure the rice and water properly. In addition, there are two differences between cooking sushi rice and cooking regular rice. First, the soaking time for sushi rice is shorter when you cook it in a deep pan. If you use a rice cooker, you should cook sushi rice with a little bit less water (about 1 tablespoon less) than when you cook regular white rice because the rice cooker includes soaking time in the cooking process. This is important because you don't want the rice to get too mushy during mixing and shaping. Second, you should cook sushi rice with dried kelp to add great umami flavor to the rice.

Sushi Rice

Makes 4 cups
(4 big rolls or
8 thin rolls
or 48 pieces
nigiri sushi)

PREP TIME:
25 minutes

COOK TIME:
25 minutes

Here I teach you how to make sushi rice in a pan. The taste of sushi rice varies depending on the rice and vinegar mixture. In this recipe, you will learn how to make a great vinegar mixture and how to balance the flavors to make delicious sushi rice! If you want, however, the amount of sugar in the mixture can be increased or decreased.

1½ cups short-grain white rice

1⅔ cups water

3 tablespoons rice vinegar

5 teaspoons sugar

2 teaspoons salt

1 (4-by-4-inch) piece dried kelp (dashi kombu)

1. In a fine-mesh strainer set atop a bowl, rinse the rice under cool running water while stirring it with your hand. Drain the rice as soon as the water in the bowl turns a murky white color. Repeat until the water in the bowl is clear.

2. In a medium bowl, combine the rice and water and let soak for 15 minutes at room temperature.

3. In a small bowl, mix the rice vinegar, sugar, and salt. Set aside.

4. Pour the rice and water into a deep saucepan and add the kelp. Cover the pan and bring the mixture to a boil over high heat. Turn the heat to low and cook for 10 minutes. When there is no water left in the pan, turn off the heat, put a kitchen towel under the lid, and steam the rice for 10 minutes.

5. Remove the kelp and discard. Transfer the rice to a large mixing bowl. Add the vinegar mixture to the bowl. Using a rice paddle, fold gently to combine and coat each grain of rice with the mixture (it is like mixing whipped egg whites into cake batter). Cover with a damp, clean cloth and allow to cool to room temperature before using the rice to make sushi.

CONTINUED

COOKING TIP: Before putting a kitchen towel over the rice, check inside the pan. If there is still water visible in the pan, put the lid back on and cook for 2 more minutes, then check again.

STORAGE TIP: Transfer the sushi rice to a freezer bag or glass container. Keep in the freezer and use within 3 weeks. To thaw it, microwave the rice on a microwave-safe plate, covered, for 2 to 3 minutes. For storing in the refrigerator, transfer the sushi rice to a clean container, cover, and refrigerate. Use within half a day.

HOW TO AVOID MISSHAPEN SUSHI ROLLS

A common problem sushi beginners experience when making sushi rolls is that the sushi nori sheet cracks, doesn't close, or falls apart. Here are some great solutions for these issues:

- Spread the sushi rice on the nori sheet properly. I recommend spreading 1 cup of sushi rice on a whole nori sheet (or ½ cup of sushi rice on a half nori sheet). This amount will fluctuate a little depending on the recipe. It takes a little practice to spread the rice evenly. If there is too much or too little rice, the roll won't close or will be too loose. Therefore, for beginners, I highly recommend that you spread the rice on the nori sheet gradually until you can't see the nori between the grains of rice.

- Choose the proper amount of filling and don't overfill. Too much filling causes sushi rolls to crack or open. Basically, for a thin roll, start with the filling in a tight pile on the rice. The height of the pile of filling should be less than one-quarter of the length of the short side of the nori sheet.

- Roll tightly. Even when the amount of rice and filling are adequate, if you roll loosely, the rolls won't hold together.

- Make sushi rolls a lot. Practice leads to mastery.

FOOD SAFETY: Because sushi contains raw fish and vegetables, it is very important to wash your hands frequently and to use different cutting boards for each kind of ingredient (fish, shellfish, vegetables).

Preparing Seafood

Here are helpful instructions on how to thaw and cut seafood to make a great final presentation. The exact cutting processes suggested here are not absolutely required, but you will have a much easier time making sushi when you follow these directions.

SASHIMI-GRADE TUNA AND SALMON

1. To thaw, place unpackaged frozen fillets on a plate, cover, and refrigerate for about 10 hours.

2. To remove fishy odor, wash the fillets quickly under running water and gently pat dry with paper towels.

3. Cut at a right angle to the grain. For sashimi dishes, slice into approximately 1-by-2-inch pieces that are ⅓ inch thick (1). For nigiri sushi, slice in approximately 1-by-2-inch pieces that are ¼ inch thick (2). For sushi rolls, cut the fish into ½-inch-thick and 2½-inch-long sticks (3). When cutting fish for all types of sushi, carefully pull the knife toward you in one motion so the fillet doesn't tear.

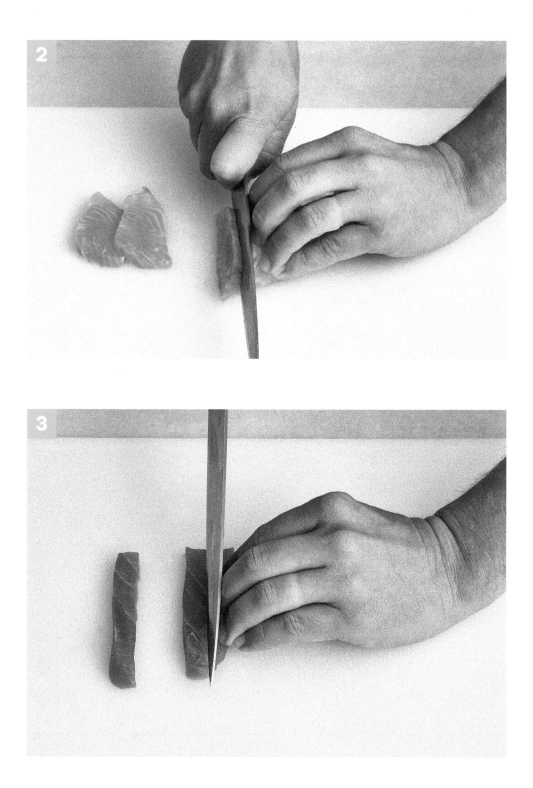

SHRIMP

1. If the shrimp are frozen, soak in salt water (1 tablespoon salt per 2 cups water) and keep in the refrigerator for 1 to 2 hours to thaw.

2. In a bowl, place the thawed shrimp (regardless of whether the shell is on or off) and sprinkle with baking soda (2 tablespoons baking soda per pound). Toss to coat for 1 minute and rinse well with water. Lay the shrimp on paper towels and use more paper towels to blot.

3. Cut the tip of the tail off (if it is tail-on) and scrape off the water on the tail with a knife. This helps remove the fishy smell and avoid oil splatters when it is fried.

4. For nigiri sushi, use shell-on, tail-on, un-deveined medium-size shrimp. For sushi rolls, use deveined medium or large shrimp. If you prefer that the tail stick out from your sushi roll for final presentation, choose tail-on shrimp.

SCALLOPS

1. To thaw, place unpackaged frozen scallops on a plate, cover, and keep in the refrigerator for 4 to 5 hours.

2. Pat the thawed scallops dry with a paper towel. Do not rinse with water, because scallops can become bland easily.

3. For sashimi dishes, halve the scallops horizontally. For nigiri sushi, make an incision from the side and butterfly.

SALMON ROE

Store-bought jarred salmon roe basically does not require preparation. But taste it before serving. If you find the taste is too salty, you can soak the roe in salt water (1 teaspoon salt per 1 cup water) for about 30 minutes. Drain and gently pat dry with a paper towel.

Preparing Vegetables and Other Common Items

In this section I will teach you handy methods for preparing sushi vegetables and other common items used in making sushi.

CUCUMBER

Use Persian cucumber (baby cucumber) that has low moisture, so the sushi roll doesn't become soggy. For sushi rolls, halve lengthwise, then halve lengthwise again to make sticks. To use cucumber to cover a sushi roll as a topping, slice lengthwise with a peeler or slicer. For garnishing sashimi dishes, slice diagonally or use a small cookie cutter to make decorative shapes.

AVOCADO

For sushi rolls, cut into quarters lengthwise, remove the pit, peel, and slice length-wise. For use as a topping, cut in half lengthwise and remove the pit. Using the knife tip, score the avocado flesh without piercing the skin and scoop it out with a spoon.

LEAF LETTUCE

Wash each leaf and pat dry with a paper towel. For thin sushi rolls, halve length-wise. For big rolls, if the leaf is shorter than the sushi nori, use without cutting. For garnishing sashimi dishes, tear into palm-sized pieces and lay some sashimi on the lettuce.

IMITATION CRABMEAT

For sushi rolls, halve lengthwise if the imitation crabmeat is leg-style. When the imitation crabmeat is flaked, cut into ½-inch pieces.

DAIKON RADISH

For garnishing sashimi dishes, shred thinly. Traditionally, daikon should be prepared like a zucchini noodle. The surface of a ½-inch-thick columnar daikon radish should be spirally stripped toward the center (this is called *katsuramuki*), then the daikon sheet should be cut so it looks like a noodle. Lay some sashimi on the shredded daikon.

SUSHI NORI

Place the nori shiny-side down and put sushi rice on the rough side of the nori. For thick (big) sushi rolls, use a whole sheet (about 7 by 8 inches). For thin rolls, halve the sheet on the long side. For *gunkanmaki*, cut the long side of the sheet into six equal lengths. For hand-rolled sushi, cut the sheet into quarters so each piece of nori is approximately square.

CHAPTER

3

Sashimi, Nigiri, and Other Sushi Dishes

THIS CHAPTER INTRODUCES A VARIETY OF SASHIMI AND sushi dishes ranging from the traditional to the creative. For a long time, Japanese people believed that certain sushi dishes are purely restaurant food, and therefore these dishes were rarely made at home. But in recent times the sushi boom around the world has made Japanese people rethink this conventional idea, and they have begun cooking more sushi dishes at home. In fact, a number of "sushi cooking kits" are now on sale in Japan, but using my recipes, you can make delicious sushi without any special tools.

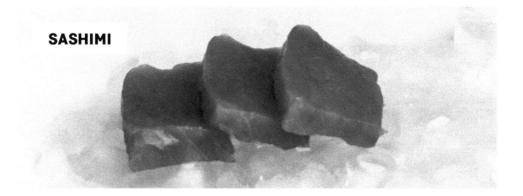

SASHIMI

Assorted Sashimi

GLUTEN-FREE,
NUT-FREE,
PESCATARIAN

Makes
8 pieces

PREP TIME:
10 minutes

This signature sashimi dish contains tuna, salmon, and seared bonito. The dish is served all over Japan with wasabi and a small dish of soy sauce. In this recipe, each fillet is ½ pound and makes about 4 servings. It is often used as a side dish. If you go to a sushi restaurant or izakaya (dining bar) in Japan, you will often see people enjoying this simple and delightful dish.

¼ small daikon radish, shredded

1 green leaf lettuce leaf, torn

1 teaspoon wasabi

½ pound sashimi-grade tuna, sliced

½ pound sashimi-grade salmon, sliced

½ pound seared bonito, sliced in ⅓-inch-wide pieces

Soy sauce (gluten-free if necessary)

1. Line a serving plate with the daikon, arrange the lettuce on the daikon, and make the wasabi into a mound on the corner.

2. Place the sliced tuna, salmon, and bonito on the lettuce.

3. Serve with a small, shallow dish of soy sauce for each person.

SUBSTITUTION TIP: If you can find Japanese **shiso** (perilla), substitute it for green leaf lettuce.

SASHIMI

Auspicious Sashimi

**GLUTEN-FREE,
NUT-FREE,
PESCATARIAN**

**Makes
4 pieces**

PREP TIME:
10 minutes

This is a scallop and salmon roe sashimi dish eaten without soy sauce. Natural sea salt brings out the flavor of the fresh scallop. To eat, dredge the scallop in a very small amount of salt. To serve salmon roe as a sashimi dish, place it in a small, deep plate, like a sake cup. You can eat the roe with chopsticks or a small spoon.

1 green leaf lettuce leaf, torn into 4 pieces

4 sashimi-grade scallops, halved horizontally

1 teaspoon natural sea salt

4 tablespoons salmon roe

Wasabi

1. Line a serving plate with lettuce, put 2 slices of scallop on each piece of lettuce, and place the salt on the corner of the plate.

2. Place 1 tablespoon of salmon roe on a deep, small plate and put a dash of wasabi on top. Repeat for three more plates with the remaining salmon roe and wasabi.

SUBSTITUTION TIP: If you can find Japanese shiso (perilla), substitute it for the green leaf lettuce.

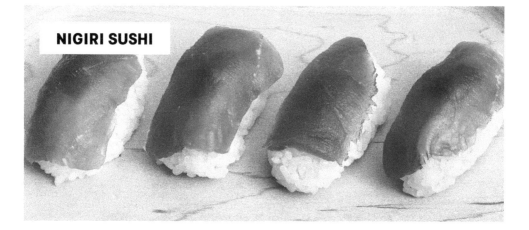

NIGIRI SUSHI

Maguro (Tuna) Nigiri

GLUTEN-FREE,
NUT-FREE,
PESCATARIAN

Makes 10 to
12 pieces

PREP TIME:
20 minutes

Bright-red, fresh maguro is tantalizing and has a light taste, so it is a great nigiri starter. Nonfat maguro (which is not toro) is very healthy. It is low in calories (3 slices of maguro have about 40 kcal) and high in protein, vitamin B, and vitamin D. The prep time is 20 minutes, but it may become shorter once you get used to making the proper shape with the nigiri sushi rice.

2 cups Sushi Rice (page 17)

Wasabi

½ pound sashimi-grade
tuna, sliced

2 tablespoons Pickled Sushi
Ginger (page 163)

Soy sauce (gluten-free if
necessary)

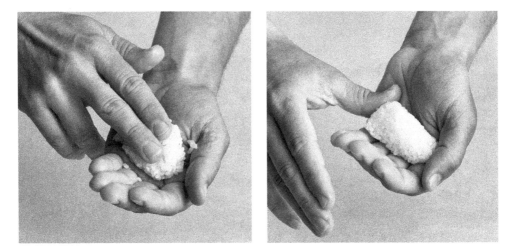

1. Scoop 1 heaping tablespoon of sushi rice on your wet hand and make it into a flat football shape.

CONTINUED

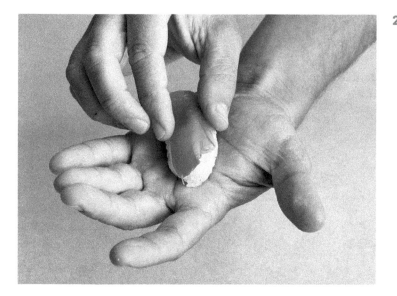

2. Place a dash of wasabi on the center of the rice, cover with a slice of tuna, gently press the fish down on the rice, and transfer it to a serving plate. Repeat with the remaining rice, wasabi, and tuna.

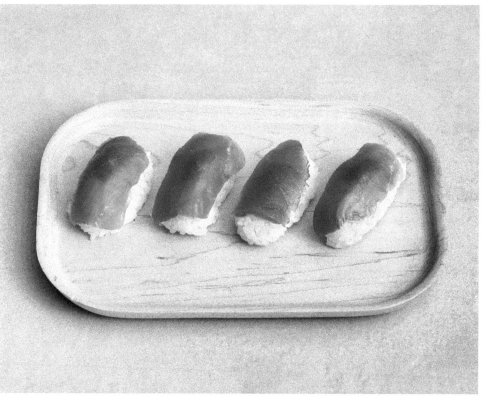

3. Put the ginger on the corner of the plate (or in a small bowl alongside) and serve with a small, shallow dish of soy sauce for each person.

COOKING TIP: Wet your hands and the tablespoon before touching the sushi rice so the rice doesn't stick.

INGREDIENT TIP: If you prefer not to use wasabi, skip that part of the step.

Salmon Nigiri with Marinated Sweet Onion

**GLUTEN-FREE,
NUT-FREE,
PESCATARIAN**

Makes 10 to
12 pieces

PREP TIME:
20 minutes

This traditional salmon nigiri sushi is eaten with marinated onion rather than wasabi. The onion's pungent component, which comes from allyl sulfide, refreshes the palate when it is eaten with rich and fatty-tasting fish. Also, the allyl sulfide helps our bodies absorb vitamin B_1, which enables the body to use carbohydrates for energy. The combination of salmon and onion is great, because salmon is high in vitamin B_1.

2 cups Sushi Rice (page 17)

½ pound sashimi-grade salmon, sliced

¼ cup Marinated Sweet Onion (page 137)

Soy sauce (gluten-free if necessary)

1. Scoop 1 heaping tablespoon of sushi rice on your wet hand and make it into a flat football shape.

2. Place a slice of salmon on the rice and top with 1 teaspoon of onion. Repeat with the remaining rice, salmon, and onion.

3. Serve with a small, shallow dish of soy sauce for each person.

Japanese Egg Omelet Nigiri

**GLUTEN-FREE,
NUT-FREE,
KID FRIENDLY,
VEGETARIAN**

**Makes
10 pieces**

PREP TIME:
20 minutes

This is a popular nigiri in sushi restaurants despite the fact that it is a nonseafood sushi. Also, most kids love it because egg omelets are a dish that kids usually enjoy and the sushi is served without wasabi. The egg omelet is usually shaky on the sushi rice, so it is fastened using a nori strip. But traditionally, this nigiri sushi is served either with and without the nori. When the omelet stays firmly on top of the rice, it is not necessary to use nori.

2 cups Sushi Rice (page 17)

Japanese Egg Omelet
(page 144), cut crosswise into
ten ½-inch-wide pieces

10 (½-by-4-inch) nori strips

Soy sauce (gluten-free if
necessary)

1. Divide the rice into 10 portions, place each into wet hands, and make into a flat football shape.

2. Place a piece of omelet on each piece of shaped rice.

3. Fasten the omelet in place using one nori strip crossways with the seam on the bottom. Place the sushi seam-side down on a serving plate. Repeat with the remaining rice, omelet pieces, and nori strips.

4. Serve with a small, shallow dish of soy sauce for each person.

Scallop Nigiri

**GLUTEN-FREE,
NUT-FREE,
PESCATARIAN**

**Makes
10 pieces**

PREP TIME:
20 minutes

*As with the scallop sashimi dish, scallop nigiri sushi is served
with natural sea salt. This is a special way to eat it, but only
when the scallop is very fresh. You can use soy sauce instead
of salt if you prefer the taste or if the scallop is not very fresh.
The scallop is butterflied and placed on top of the sushi rice. If
you halve the scallop by accident, you can lay half the sliced
scallop overlapping the edge of the other half on the rice.*

2 cups Sushi Rice (page 17)

Wasabi

10 scallops, butterflied

2 tablespoons Pickled Sushi
Ginger (page 163)

Natural sea salt

1. Divide the rice into 10 portions, place each into wet hands, and
   make into a flat football shape.

2. Place a dash of wasabi on the center of the rice, cover with a
   scallop, and transfer to a serving plate. Repeat with the remaining rice, wasabi, and scallops.

3. Put the ginger on the corner of the plate and serve with a small,
   shallow dish of salt for each person.

Boiled Shrimp Nigiri

GLUTEN-FREE, NUT-FREE, PESCATARIAN

Makes 10 pieces

PREP TIME: 35 minutes

COOK TIME: 5 minutes

The tail-on pink-shrimp makes this dish great looking. To make boiled nigiri sushi shrimp perfectly, you should choose tail-on, un-deveined, medium-size shrimp. Store-bought deveined shrimp is usually slit on the back side, which makes it impossible to butterfly the shrimp from the belly side. You can butterfly the shrimp from the back side, but the tail becomes upswept (meaning upside down) when it lays on the rice. Large shrimp can be used as nigiri sushi shrimp, but it is a little bit difficult to butterfly them because of their thickness.

10 medium shell-on, tail-on shrimp, prepared (see page 21)

2 cups Sushi Rice (page 17)

Wasabi

Soy sauce (gluten-free if necessary)

1. Fill a deep pan with water and bring it to a boil over high heat.

2. Meanwhile, slowly insert a skewer in the shrimp from head to tail beneath the shell on the belly (leg) side to prevent it from curling when cooked. Boil five skewered shrimp at a time over medium heat for 2 to 3 minutes, or until they turn pink.

3. Once it cools enough to handle, remove the shell and legs, and make an incision from the belly side and butterfly. After it is opened, if you see back veins, gently remove them.

4. Divide the rice into 10 portions. With wet hands, form each portion into a flat football shape.

5. Place a dash of wasabi on the center of the rice and cover with a piece of shrimp. Repeat with the remaining rice, wasabi, and shrimp.

6. Serve with a small, shallow dish of soy sauce for each person.

COOKING TIP: You can devein shrimp using a toothpick without cutting, but this requires a little technique. For nigiri shrimp, it is easiest to devein after butterflying.

Beef with Scallion Nigiri

GLUTEN-FREE, NUT-FREE

Makes 10 to 12 pieces

PREP TIME:
20 minutes

COOK TIME:
10 minutes

Although traditional sushi is a combination of seafood and rice, there are now many other types of sushi. This beef nigiri has become very popular in sushi restaurants in Japan. The beef is seasoned with soy sauce and wasabi, so the taste goes really well with sushi rice. It is also a great idea to use roasted beef instead of sautéed beef if you like.

6 ounces sirloin steak, chuck steak, or rib eye steak, sliced into 1-by-2-inch pieces, ¼ to ½ inch thick

¼ teaspoon wasabi

1 tablespoon soy sauce (gluten-free if necessary)

2 cups Sushi Rice (page 17)

2 scallions, both white and green parts, chopped

1. Heat a dry skillet over medium heat for a few minutes, then cook the beef on one side for 3 to 4 minutes.

2. Meanwhile, mix the wasabi and soy sauce.

3. Flip the beef, add the sauce, and cook for another 3 to 4 minutes, until it turns brown. Set aside.

4. Scoop 1 heaping tablespoon of sushi rice on your wet hand and make it into a flat football shape. Repeat with the remaining rice.

5. Once the beef cools enough to handle, place a piece on each mound of shaped rice, transfer to a serving dish, and sprinkle with the scallions.

COOKING TIP: If the skillet is too small to cook all the beef at once, cook it in batches.

INGREDIENT TIP: If you use leaner meat, heat ½ tablespoon oil in the skillet until it shimmers before adding the beef to the pan.

Chicken Teriyaki Nigiri

GLUTEN-FREE, NUT-FREE, KID FRIENDLY

Makes 10 to 12 pieces

PREP TIME: 25 minutes

COOK TIME: 15 minutes

This nigiri is very popular with kids. Chicken teriyaki is a common food from Japan. It has a sweet-savory taste and a juicy, soft texture. Homemade chicken teriyaki takes only 15 minutes using one skillet. The key to making juicy chicken in a short amount of time is panfrying and pan-steaming the chicken with cooking sake. If you prefer, you can use any kind of broth instead of sake. Because of the shape of the sliced chicken, you need to fasten the chicken onto the sushi rice using a nori strip.

1 tablespoon vegetable oil

2 medium boneless, skinless chicken thighs

½ tablespoon cooking sake, plus 1 teaspoon

½ tablespoon soy sauce (gluten-free if necessary)

½ tablespoon mirin

½ teaspoon sugar

2 cups Sushi Rice (page 17)

10 (½-by-4-inch) nori strips

1. In a skillet, heat the vegetable oil over medium heat until it shimmers. Add the chicken and cook for 4 minutes. Flip the chicken, add ½ tablespoon of cooking sake, cover the skillet, and reduce the heat to low. Steam the chicken for 3 minutes.

2. Add the remaining 1 teaspoon of cooking sake, the soy sauce, mirin, and sugar. Increase the heat to medium and simmer for 6 minutes, turning the chicken occasionally and using a spoon to baste it with the sauce frequently, until the sauce is almost completely reduced. Let it cool and slice into ½-inch-thick pieces.

3. Scoop 1 heaping tablespoon of sushi rice onto your wet hand and make it into a flat football shape. Place a piece of chicken on the rice. Fasten the chicken in place using 1 nori strip crossways with the seam on the bottom. Place the sushi seam-side down on a serving plate. Repeat with the remaining rice, chicken, and nori.

Spam Nigiri

GLUTEN-FREE, NUT-FREE, KID FRIENDLY

Makes 10 pieces

PREP TIME: 25 minutes

COOK TIME: 5 minutes

Believe it or not, Spam is very popular in Japan, especially in the Okinawa islands, because the main island has many US military bases. Spam is a great emergency food because under the right conditions, it lasts three years from the production date, and it can be eaten on its own. In fact, in the aftermath of the Great East Japan Earthquake (2011), Spam was issued for disaster victims. Japanese people use Spam mainly as an ingredient for sautéed dishes, rice balls, sandwiches, and fried rice.

1 (12-ounce) can Spam, sliced into 10 pieces

2 cups Sushi Rice (page 17)

10 (½-by-4-inch) nori strips

1. Heat a dry skillet over medium heat for a few minutes, then cook the Spam for 3 to 4 minutes, flipping halfway through the cooking time, until it is browned.

2. Divide the rice into 10 portions. Place each portion into wet hands, and make into a flat football shape.

3. Fasten the Spam in place using 1 nori strip crossways with the seam on the bottom. Place the sushi seam-side down on a serving plate. Repeat with the remaining rice, Spam, and nori.

INARI SUSHI

Simple Inari Sushi

NUT-FREE,
VEGAN

Makes
16 pieces

PREP TIME:
25 minutes

Inari sushi is sweet–savory fried bean curd stuffed with sushi rice, and it is often a homemade sushi dish in Japan. It is not usually seen in fancy sushi restaurants. This recipe is a simple style of inari that is stuffed with sushi rice mixed with sesame seeds, which is popular in eastern Japan. Because the bean curd is already seasoned and delicious, inari is eaten without any sauce. In Japan, people usually cook the inari fried bean curd from scratch using fried tofu skin, but here I use prepared bean curd available on Amazon or your local Asian market to make the recipe easier.

1 (10-ounce) can Inarizushi No
Moto Bean Curd

4 cups Sushi Rice (page 17)

2 tablespoons roasted
sesame seeds

1. Drain the canned fried bean curd. Squeeze each piece in your palms gently and lightly. On a work surface, open each piece carefully by hand (like opening a pita).

2. In a bowl, mix the sushi rice and the sesame seeds.

3. Carefully stuff 2 tablespoons of the rice mixture into each opened bean curd and place it open-side down on a serving plate.

COOKING TIP: The fried bean curd is very thin and breakable. Treat it with care when opening and stuffing.

INARI SUSHI

Vegetable Inari Sushi

NUT-FREE, VEGAN

Makes 16 pieces

PREP TIME: 30 minutes

COOK TIME: 15 minutes

This inari sushi is stuffed with rice mixed with simmered shiitake mushroom and carrot. It is popular in western Japan. For a good final presentation, the inari is placed rice-side up on a serving plate because the vegetables give the dish a beautiful color. Inari traditionally doesn't include raw fish, but nowadays it is occasionally topped with salmon roe. In that case, a small amount of salmon roe (about 1 teaspoon) is put on the rice side of the inari.

5 small shiitake mushrooms, stemmed and finely chopped

1 small carrot, finely chopped

1 teaspoon Shimaya kombu dashi soup stock powder or any dashi powder you like

2 tablespoons soy sauce

1 tablespoon cooking sake

2 tablespoons sugar

½ teaspoon salt

⅔ cup water

1 (10-ounce) can Inarizushi No Moto Bean Curd

4 cups Sushi Rice (page 17)

1. In a saucepan, stir together the mushrooms, carrot, dashi powder, soy sauce, cooking sake, sugar, salt, and water. Bring to a boil over medium heat, reduce the heat to maintain a simmer, and cook for 10 minutes. Let cool, then drain the vegetables.

2. Meanwhile, drain the canned fried bean curd. Squeeze each piece in your palms gently and lightly. Open each piece carefully by hand (like opening a pita).

3. In a bowl, combine the rice and the vegetables and mix well.

4. Carefully stuff 2 tablespoons of the rice and vegetable mixture into each opened bean curd and place each piece open-side up on a serving plate.

GUNKANMAKI SUSHI

Salmon Roe (Ikura) Gunkanmaki

GLUTEN-FREE, NUT-FREE, PESCATARIAN

Makes 10 to 12 pieces

PREP TIME: 30 minutes

Gunkan *means "warship" in Japanese. Gunkanmaki is so named because the warship shape is great for holding ingredients that would be easily dropped in any other form. Salmon roe (ikura) has a rich umami taste. It is high in good protein, vitamins, and magnesium. Most notably, in fish and shellfish, ikura is one of the best arginine-rich foods, which are known to boost your immune system. It is healthy, but it is also high in calories and cholesterol, so be sure to eat only a small portion.*

2 cups Sushi Rice (page 17)

2 whole nori sheets, cut (see page 23)

7 ounces salmon roe

1. Scoop 1 heaping tablespoon of sushi rice on your wet hand and form it into a flat football shape.

2. Wrap a strip of nori around the sides of the rice, shiny-side out, creating a tiny collar all around the rice. It is okay that the edge of the nori strip doesn't stick firmly.

3. Place 1 tablespoon of salmon roe on top of the rice. Repeat with the remaining rice, nori, and salmon roe.

Minced Tuna and Scallion (Negitoro) Gunkanmaki

GLUTEN-FREE, NUT-FREE, PESCATARIAN

Makes 12 pieces

PREP TIME: 40 minutes

Negitoro means scallion (negi) and fatty tuna (toro) in Japanese. Even though the recipe uses lean tuna, it is called toro because minced tuna has a fluffy texture and it seems to melt in your mouth like toro. Sometimes the tuna is seasoned with mayonnaise for the recipe in Japan, but here I introduce you to the traditional recipe using soy sauce.

½ pound sashimi-grade tuna

1 tablespoon soy sauce (gluten-free if necessary)

2 cups Sushi Rice (page 17)

2 whole nori sheets, cut (see page 23)

1 scallion, both white and green parts, chopped

1. Cut the tuna into small pieces and mince finely. Place in a bowl, mix in the soy sauce, and divide into 12 equal portions.

CONTINUED

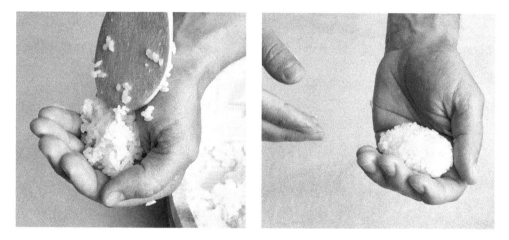

2. Divide the rice into 12 portions, place each portion into your wet hand, and make into a flat football shape.

3. Wrap a strip of nori around the sides of the rice, shiny-side out, creating a tiny collar all around the rice. It is okay that the edge of the nori strip doesn't stick firmly.

4. Put one portion of the tuna mixture on the rice and top with some chopped scallion. Repeat with the remaining rice, nori, tuna, and scallions.

GUNKANMAKI SUSHI

Lemony Crabmeat Gunkanmaki

**GLUTEN-FREE,
NUT-FREE,
PESCATARIAN**

**Makes 10 to
12 pieces**

PREP TIME:
40 minutes

This gunkanmaki is great for eating crabmeat as a sushi dish because lump crab is hard to use in other types of sushi. In this recipe the crabmeat is seasoned with lemon juice, salt, and pepper. If you prefer, it can be seasoned with mayonnaise instead of lemon juice. The sliced cucumber adds a nice touch to the sushi. Sometimes the piece of cucumber in gunkanmaki is used to brush the sushi with soy sauce if needed; just dip the edge of the cucumber in soy sauce and brush over the sushi.

1 (4¼-ounce) can lump
crabmeat, drained

Salt

Freshly ground black pepper

Juice of ½ lemon

2 cups Sushi Rice (page 17)

2 whole nori sheets, cut
(see page 23)

1 baby cucumber, sliced
diagonally

1. In a bowl, whisk together the crabmeat, a pinch of salt and pepper, and lemon juice. Taste and add more salt and pepper as needed.

2. Scoop 1 heaping tablespoon of sushi rice on your wet hand and form into a flat football shape.

3. Wrap a strip of nori around the sides of the rice, shiny-side out, creating a tiny collar all around the rice. It is okay that the edge of the nori strip doesn't stick firmly.

4. Set 1 or 2 pieces of sliced cucumber on the edge of the rice, and put 2 teaspoons of the crabmeat on the rice. Repeat with the remaining rice, nori, cucumber, and crabmeat.

Buttery Corn Gunkanmaki

GLUTEN-FREE, NUT-FREE, VEGETARIAN, KID FRIENDLY

Makes 10 to 12 pieces

PREP TIME: 30 minutes

COOK TIME: 10 minutes

This dish is very popular with kids. It is not a traditional recipe, but nowadays this sushi can be found at most conveyor-belt sushi restaurants in Japan. Butter and soy sauce add a rich flavor to the dish. I use frozen corn, but fresh corn can also be used for this recipe. In that case, cook the corn over medium-low heat instead, for about 5 minutes.

2 tablespoons butter or margarine

1 cup frozen sweet corn kernels

2 tablespoons soy sauce (gluten-free if necessary)

2 cups Sushi Rice (page 17)

2 whole nori sheets, cut (see page 23)

1. In a skillet, melt the butter over medium-high heat. Add the corn and stir-fry for about 5 minutes to evaporate the water from the frozen corn. Add the soy sauce and stir for 1 minute.

2. Scoop 1 heaping tablespoon of sushi rice on your wet hand and form it into a flat football shape.

3. Wrap a strip of nori around the sides of the rice, shiny-side out, creating a tiny collar all around the rice. It is okay that the edge of the nori strip doesn't stick firmly.

4. Put 1 tablespoon of the corn on top. Repeat with the remaining rice, nori, and corn.

Corn and Tuna with Mayo Gunkanmaki

NUT-FREE,
PESCATARIAN,
KID FRIENDLY

Makes 10 to
12 pieces

PREP TIME:
30 minutes

COOK TIME:
1 minute

This combination of corn and tuna is very popular in Japan. There is a canned product sold in Japan that is a tuna and corn mixture. We use it for sautéed dishes, salad, pasta, pizza, and rice dishes. In this recipe, corn and tuna are seasoned with mayonnaise. I always have frozen corn in my freezer because it is very handy. I use it for this recipe as well, but you can substitute fresh corn kernels. This sushi is served at many sushi restaurants and is enjoyed by people of all ages.

½ cup frozen sweet
corn kernels

1 (5-ounce) can tuna packed in
water, drained

2 tablespoons mayonnaise

Salt

Freshly ground black pepper

2 cups Sushi Rice (page 17)

2 whole nori sheets, cut (see
page 23)

1. In a small microwave-safe bowl, microwave the frozen corn, covered, for about 50 seconds.

2. In a small bowl, mix the corn, tuna, and mayonnaise. Taste and season with salt and pepper as needed.

3. Scoop 1 heaping tablespoon of sushi rice on your wet hand and form it into a flat football shape.

4. Wrap a strip of nori around the sides of the rice, shiny-side out, creating a tiny collar all around the rice. It is okay that the edge of the nori strip doesn't stick firmly.

5. Put 1 tablespoon of the tuna mixture on top. Repeat with the remaining rice, nori, and tuna mixture.

CHIRASHI SUSHI

Vegetable Chirashi (Gomoku Chirashi)

GLUTEN-FREE,
NUT-FREE,
VEGETARIAN

Serves 4

PREP TIME:
10 minutes

COOK TIME:
20 minutes

Gomoku chirashi is traditionally homemade food and served on the Japanese Girls' Day holiday, which is on March 3 each year. The ingredients vary considerably from one region to another. Sometimes it is topped with boiled shrimp or cooked eel. Here I introduce a gomoku chirashi recipe without meat or seafood. The basic rule of a traditional Japanese diet is ichi-juu san-sai, which means that a meal should consist of one bowl of cooked rice, one kind of soup, and three side dishes. The chirashi dish has been said to combine all these dishes (except the soup) in one bowl so it is usually served alone or with soup.

5 small shiitake mushrooms, stemmed and cut into small pieces

1 small carrot, cut into small pieces

1 teaspoon Shimaya kombu dashi soup stock powder or any dashi powder you like

2 tablespoons soy sauce (gluten-free if necessary)

1 tablespoon cooking sake

2 tablespoons sugar

½ teaspoon salt

⅔ cup water

Nonstick cooking spray

1 egg, beaten

4 cups Sushi Rice (page 17)

2 scallions, both white and green parts, chopped

CONTINUED

1. In a saucepan, stir together the mushrooms, carrot, dashi powder, soy sauce, cooking sake, sugar, salt, and water. Bring to a boil over medium heat, reduce the heat to maintain a simmer, and cook for 10 minutes. Let it cool, then drain.

2. Meanwhile, heat a 10-inch skillet over medium heat and coat with cooking spray. Pour the beaten egg into the skillet and spread the egg all over the surface of the pan to make a thin layer. Cook over medium-low heat for 3 minutes, gently flipping halfway through the cooking time with a rubber spatula. Once it is cool enough to touch, transfer to a cutting board, roll it up, and cut into very thin strips.

3. In a bowl, combine the rice and the vegetables and mix well. Transfer to a serving plate and top with the sliced fried egg and the scallions.

COOKING TIP: The fried egg is sliced into thin strips and used for garnish, so it is okay if the egg breaks during cooking.

Deluxe Sashimi Chirashi (Kaisen Chirashi)

GLUTEN-FREE, NUT-FREE, PESCATARIAN

Serves 4

PREP TIME: 20 minutes

This may be a familiar dish to you because it is served at many sushi restaurants outside of Japan. If you have any other sashimi in your refrigerator, it is great to add it to this dish. The difference between chirashi and a rice bowl dish is the rice itself. Chirashi always uses sushi rice under the toppings and rice bowls use unseasoned rice. For good flavor and safety, top the rice with the sashimi right before serving. Even if the dish is stored in the refrigerator, the rice gets soaked with moisture and a fishy smell from the seafood and develops a bad flavor.

4 cups Sushi Rice (page 17)

2 tablespoons roasted sesame seeds

1 baby cucumber, sliced

½ pound sashimi-grade tuna, sliced in about ¼-inch-wide pieces

½ pound sashimi-grade salmon, sliced in about ¼-inch-wide pieces

4 sashimi-grade scallops, halved horizontally

4 tablespoons salmon roe

Soy sauce (gluten-free if necessary)

2 tablespoons Pickled Sushi Ginger (page 163)

Wasabi

1. In a bowl, combine the rice and sesame seeds and mix well. Divide into four portions and transfer each to a serving plate.

2. Line one-quarter of the sliced cucumber on each rice portion and top with about three pieces each of tuna and salmon, two pieces of scallop, and 1 tablespoon of salmon roe.

3. Serve with three separate shallow dishes of soy sauce, ginger, and wasabi for each person.

SUSHI CANAPÉS

Tricolor Sushi Canapés

GLUTEN-FREE,
NUT-FREE

Makes
15 pieces

PREP TIME:
30 minutes

COOK TIME:
30 minutes

This is a great new sushi idea created by my dear friend Hitomi, a food coordinator, who recommended this dish when I asked her what I should cook for my husband. In this recipe, I use flaked salmon, chicken teriyaki crumble, and avocado with wasabi soy sauce as toppings. This dish doesn't need to be served with soy sauce, because the toppings are delicious even without it.

FOR THE TOPPINGS

1 (4- to 5-ounce) salmon fillet

1 tablespoon sesame oil

½ teaspoon salt

¼ pound ground chicken

4 tablespoons soy sauce (gluten-free if necessary), divided

1 tablespoon cooking sake

1 tablespoon mirin

1 tablespoon sugar

¼ teaspoon wasabi

1 small avocado, cubed

FOR THE SUSHI CANAPÉS

3 whole nori sheets

3 cups Sushi Rice (page 17)

TO MAKE THE TOPPINGS

1. Fill a medium saucepan with water and bring it to a boil over high heat. Reduce the heat to medium, add the salmon, boil for 5 minutes, and drain. Using two forks, shred the cooked salmon, removing any skin and bones.

2. In a skillet, heat the sesame oil over medium heat until it shimmers. Add the shredded salmon and cook for 2 to 3 minutes, seasoning with the salt halfway through the cooking time. Set aside.

3. In another dry skillet, cook the ground chicken over medium heat for 5 minutes, breaking it up with a spoon, until it is browned and no longer pink. Drain the excess fat. Add 2 tablespoons of soy sauce, cooking sake, mirin, and sugar. Cook for 5 minutes, stirring, until the sauce is reduced. Set aside.

4. In a small bowl, mix together the remaining 2 tablespoons of soy sauce and the wasabi. Add the avocado and toss until completely coated. Set aside.

TO MAKE THE SUSHI CANAPÉS

5. Lay out the *makisu* on a work surface and place one piece of nori on it. Spread 1 cup of sushi rice over the nori. Pick up the edge of the makisu and nori closest to you, and roll into a tight jelly roll. Make two more rolls with the remaining nori and rice.

6. Cut each sushi roll into 5 pieces.

7. Put ½ tablespoon of one kind of topping on each of five canapés. Repeat with the other two toppings.

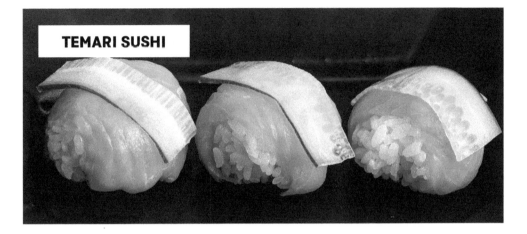
TEMARI SUSHI

Egg and Salmon Roe Temari

GLUTEN-FREE,
NUT-FREE,
PESCATARIAN

Makes
18 pieces

PREP TIME:
25 minutes

COOK TIME:
10 minutes

Temari is the name of a traditional colorful hand-sized ball, which is a Japanese craft. Therefore, temari sushi is small, cute, and ball shaped. This recipe is a hallmark of temari sushi with the rice ball wrapped in thin fried egg and topped with salmon roe. It has vibrant colors, which are yellow and orange, and the ball shape of the rice and the salmon roe match really well. This temari sushi recipe can take center stage at any party!

1 teaspoon cornstarch	Nonstick cooking spray
1 teaspoon water	3 cups Sushi Rice (page 17)
2 eggs, beaten	3 tablespoons salmon roe

1. In a small bowl, whisk together the cornstarch and water. Mix the cornstarch mixture into the beaten eggs.

2. Heat a 10-inch skillet over medium-high heat and coat with cooking spray. Pour half of the egg mixture into the skillet and spread the egg all over the surface of the pan to make a thin layer. Cook over low heat for about 3 minutes, gently flipping halfway through the cooking time with a rubber spatula. Make another thin fried egg with the remaining egg mixture.

3. Transfer the fried eggs to a cutting board, cut each lengthwise into three equal pieces, then cut each piece crosswise into three pieces to create 18 approximately equal-sized pieces.

4. On a 6-by-6-inch piece of plastic wrap or damp cheesecloth, place 1 piece of egg and scoop 1 heaping tablespoon of the rice on the egg.

5. Hold up the four corners of the wrapper with one hand and twist the sushi tightly with the other hand to make a ball shape. Transfer the sushi to a serving plate. Repeat with the remaining egg pieces and rice.

6. Top each sushi with ½ teaspoon of salmon roe.

COOKING TIP: The cornstarch keeps the thin fried egg from tearing. However, when it is cooked too long, the egg crisps and can shatter.

TEMARI SUSHI

Smoked Salmon Temari with Cucumber

GLUTEN-FREE, NUT-FREE, PESCATARIAN

Makes 12 pieces

PREP TIME: 25 minutes

Temari sushi, which is pronounced "temari-zushi" in Japanese, was created in recent years but nobody is sure exactly when. There is a theory that Kyoto, Japan's ancient imperial capital, is the birthplace of temari sushi. Temari sushi has a small, round ball shape and can be eaten without opening your mouth wide. It may be based on an ancient belief that taking big bites or laughing with a wide-open mouth were disgraceful behaviors. Lately, it is also popular as a homemade sushi dish because it is a no-muss-no-fuss dish that is very easy to shape using plastic wrap or damp cheesecloth.

12 slices smoked salmon slices, each 2 to 3 inches long

2 cups Sushi Rice (page 17)

1 baby cucumber, thinly sliced lengthwise

1. On a 6-by-6-inch piece of plastic wrap or damp cheesecloth, place 1 slice of smoked salmon. Scoop 1 heaping tablespoon of rice on the salmon.

2. Hold up the four corners of the wrapper with one hand and twist the sushi tightly with the other hand to make a ball shape. Transfer the sushi to a serving plate. Repeat with the remaining salmon slices and rice.

CONTINUED

3. Top each piece of sushi with one slice of cucumber. The sushi can be eaten on its own.

INGREDIENT TIP: If you use cheesecloth to shape the sushi, you can keep rice from sticking to it by wringing out the cloth with water after every 2 or 3 pieces you make.

SERVING TIP: Smoked salmon has a delicious taste and flavor so the sushi can be eaten on its own. Serve with a small, shallow dish of soy sauce, if necessary.

TEMARI SUSHI

Marinated Tuna (Zuke-Maguro) Temari

**GLUTEN-FREE,
NUT-FREE,
PESCATARIAN**

**Makes
12 pieces**

PREP TIME:
55 minutes

COOK TIME:
5 minutes

Zuke was the name of one of the traditional ways for storing fresh tuna when refrigerators were not widely used. Nowadays, it is used as an ingredient in sushi and rice bowls. The tuna is marinated in a slightly sweet sauce made from a mixture of soy sauce, cooking sake, and mirin, so there is no need to serve it with any sauce.

4 tablespoons soy sauce
(gluten-free if necessary)

2 tablespoons cooking sake

2 tablespoons mirin

8 ounces sashimi-grade tuna,
sliced thinly

2 cups Sushi Rice (page 17)

Roasted white sesame seeds

2 scallions, both white and
green parts, chopped

1. In a small saucepan, stir together the soy sauce, cooking sake, and mirin. Bring the mixture to a boil over medium-high heat. Turn the heat to low and cook for 3 minutes. Turn off the heat, allow the pan to cool for 1 or 2 minutes, and transfer to the refrigerator and let it cool for about 15 minutes.

2. After cooling, remove the pan from the refrigerator, add the tuna, and flip until it is coated completely with the sauce. Marinate for 20 minutes in the refrigerator.

3. On a piece of plastic wrap (about 6 by 6 inches), place 1 slice of marinated tuna; put 1 heaping tablespoon of the rice on the tuna.

4. Hold up the four corners of the wrap with one hand and twist the sushi tightly with the other hand to make a ball shape. Transfer the sushi to a serving plate. Repeat with the remaining tuna slices and rice.

5. Sprinkle with the sesame seeds and scallions.

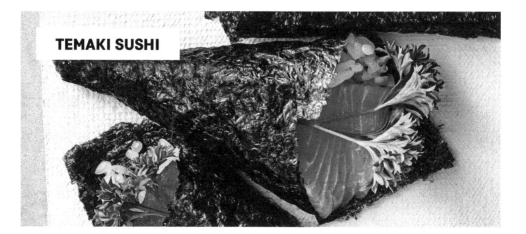

TEMAKI SUSHI

Traditional Hand-Rolled Sushi

GLUTEN-FREE, NUT-FREE, PESCATARIAN

Makes 8 rolls

PREP TIME: 40 minutes

Hand-rolled sushi, which is called temaki *in Japanese, is a traditional homemade sushi. There is no need for a special technique to roll, and you can use any ingredients you like. In this recipe I use sashimi tuna and salmon, which are the most popular ingredients for hand-rolled sushi. For temaki sushi recipes, some unseasoned ingredients are dipped in soy sauce before being set on the rice, so the sushi can be served without soy sauce. If you can get it, substitute Japanese basil (shiso) for the parsley. If you like using wasabi, put a dash of wasabi on the rice.*

2 whole nori sheets, cut (see page 23)

2 cups Sushi Rice (page 17)

¼ pound sashimi-grade tuna, sliced

¼ pound sashimi-grade salmon, sliced

Soy sauce (gluten-free if necessary)

Parsley

1. Put a piece of nori on your palm and spread 2 tablespoons rice on it with a
   wet spoon.

CONTINUED

2. Dip a piece of tuna and salmon in soy sauce, and arrange each piece with 1 sprig of parsley diagonally across the middle of the rice. Roll into a cone shape. Repeat with the remaining nori, rice, and tuna and salmon slices.

Salad Temaki

**NUT-FREE,
PESCATARIAN**

Makes 8 rolls

PREP TIME:
40 minutes

This salad hand roll is a traditional temaki sushi recipe that doesn't include any raw fish. The cucumber adds a great crunchy texture to the sushi. Leg-style imitation crabmeat is very handy and easy to use, but if you can't find it, flake-style can also be used for this recipe. In that case, use two pieces of the meat for each hand-rolled sushi. I use square nori for all hand-rolled sushi recipes. Some other recipes use rectangular nori, which is two times bigger than the square, with the same amount of rice. It is easy to make a good cone shape with rectangular nori, but the sushi has more nori and is slightly harder to bite and chew than this recipe.

Japanese Egg Omelet
(page 144)

2 whole nori sheets, cut (see page 23)

2 cups Sushi Rice (page 17)

8 pieces leg-style imitation crabmeat

1 baby cucumber, cut into thin strips

8 teaspoons mayonnaise

1. Cut the omelet into quarters lengthwise and halve each quarter crosswise. Set aside.

2. Put a piece of nori in your palm and spread 2 tablespoons of the rice over it with a wet spoon.

3. Arrange 1 piece of omelet, 1 piece of imitation crabmeat, and some sliced cucumber diagonally across the middle of the rice. Put 1 teaspoon of mayonnaise on the cucumber. Roll into a cone shape. Repeat with the remaining nori, rice, and filling.

Beef with Lettuce Temaki

GLUTEN-FREE, NUT-FREE

Makes 8 rolls

PREP TIME:
40 minutes

COOK TIME:
10 minutes

This sushi idea comes from Korean cuisine and consists of sautéed beef wrapped with lettuce. In this recipe, the vinegar-marinated sweet onion is placed on top of the beef so it has a very fresh taste. You could even use the lettuce as a wrapper instead of nori. Spread the rice on the lettuce, place the ingredients on the rice, and roll up. This is so delicious! As just described, temaki recipes are unlimited because they are easy to roll and there are no traditional rules. If you held a temaki sushi party, tons of recipes could be created by your guests!

4 ounces sirloin steak, chuck steak, or rib eye steak, cut into ½-inch-thick and 2½-inch-long stick

Salt

Freshly ground black pepper

2 whole nori sheets, cut (see page 23)

2 cups Sushi Rice (page 17)

2 green leaf lettuce leaves, torn into palm-size pieces

¼ cup Marinated Sweet Onion (page 137)

1. Heat a dry skillet over medium heat for a few minutes, and cook the beef for about 7 minutes or until it turns brown. Season with the salt and pepper halfway through the cooking time. Set aside.

2. Put a piece of nori in your palm, spread 2 tablespoons of the rice over it with a wet spoon, and place the lettuce on the rice.

3. Arrange a stick of beef and about ½ tablespoon of onion diagonally across the middle of the lettuce. Roll into a cone shape. Repeat with the remaining nori, rice, and filling.

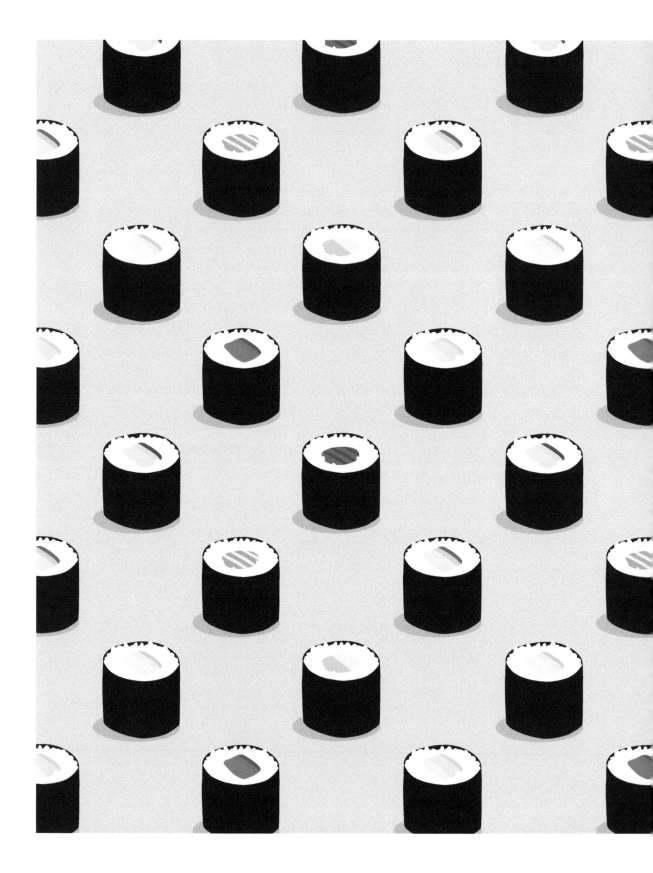

CHAPTER

4

Maki (Rolls)

MOST TRADITIONAL SUSHI ROLLS HAVE THREE SIMPLE characteristics—the outside is nori, the shape is perfectly round, and they are served without toppings. Here I will teach you how to make traditional and nontraditional rolls that are either well known or brand-new on the sushi scene.

Tuna Roll (Tekkamaki)

GLUTEN-FREE,
NUT-FREE,
PESCATARIAN

Makes 4 thin
rolls or
24 pieces

PREP TIME:
40 minutes

This thin tuna roll is a traditional and very popular dish. In Tokyo, this dish is very small and nori-side out, which makes it a handy finger food for a quick lunch. To keep things clean, I recommend using the edge of the paddle to spread the rice. Be sure to wet the paddle between each roll. See the tip for rolling technique.

2 whole nori sheets, halved

2 cups Sushi Rice (page 17)

Wasabi

4 ounces sashimi-grade tuna, cut (see page 19)

Soy sauce (gluten-free if necessary)

1. Put the *makisu* on a work surface and place one piece of nori on it, shiny-side down. Spread ½ cup of sushi rice evenly over the nori, leaving a ½-inch border visible.

2. With your finger, spread a small amount of wasabi across the middle of the rice, then lay 3 pieces of the tuna on the wasabi.

3. Begin rolling by picking up the edge of the makisu and nori closest to you and folding it over the tuna. Hold the roll tightly to form a good shape. Let it sit seam-side down for 2 minutes or until the nori sticks firmly. Make three more rolls with the remaining nori, rice, and filling.

4. Cut each sushi roll into 6 pieces with a knife that is wiped on a clean, damp kitchen towel before each cut. Transfer to a serving plate. Serve with a small shallow dish of soy sauce for each person.

COOKING TIP: Once the near side of the rice attaches to the far side of the rice, hold the roll tightly to encourage a good shape and keep it from falling apart. Then keep rolling while holding just the makisu.

Cucumber Roll (Kappamaki)

GLUTEN-FREE,
NUT-FREE,
VEGAN

Makes 4 thin
rolls or
24 pieces

PREP TIME:
40 minutes

The cucumber roll was created in Japan during a food shortage after World War II. Unexpectedly it became very popular, even though it doesn't include fresh seafood. Japanese call this roll kappamaki. *Kappa is a monster in Japanese folklore, and many kappa stories say the kappa likes to eat cucumber, so it is named kappamaki. Although the recipe notes that it takes 40 minutes to prepare, when you get used to rolling sushi, it will become faster. See the tip on page 68 for rolling technique.*

2 whole nori sheets, halved

2 cups Sushi Rice (page 17)

2 baby cucumbers, cut
(see page 22)

Soy sauce (gluten-free if
necessary)

1. Put the makisu on a work surface and place one piece of nori on it, shiny-side down. Spread ½ cup of sushi rice evenly over the nori, leaving a ½-inch border visible.

2. Place 2 sticks of cucumber across the middle of the rice.

3. Begin rolling by picking up the edge of the makisu and nori closest to you and folding it over the cucumber. Hold the roll tightly to form a good shape. Let it sit, seam-side down, for 2 minutes or until the nori sticks firmly. Make three more rolls with the remaining nori, rice, and filling.

4. Cut each sushi roll into 6 pieces with a knife that is wiped on a clean, damp kitchen towel before each cut. Transfer to a serving plate. Serve with a small shallow dish of soy sauce for each person.

COOKING TIP: This thin sushi roll can also be shaped as a square, which is a little bit easier to make. Just gently push the sides of the sushi roll against the work surface to make four flat faces while you hold the roll tightly.

Traditional Big Roll (Futomaki)

GLUTEN-FREE, NUT-FREE, VEGETARIAN

Makes 2 big rolls or 16 pieces

PREP TIME:
30 minutes

COOK TIME:
20 minutes

This sushi roll is a big roll with the nori side out and typically filled with cooked vegetables and sometimes cooked seafood. The filling has a delicious sweet and savory taste, so there is no need to eat it with any sauce. In western Japan, where I was born and raised, there is a custom to eat this roll in silence while facing the year's lucky compass direction and wishing for perfect health.

2 large shiitake mushrooms, stemmed and sliced

½ carrot, cut into ¼-inch-thick sticks

10 spinach stalks

1 teaspoon Shimaya kombu dashi soup stock powder or any dashi powder you like

⅔ cup water

2 tablespoon soy sauce (gluten-free if necessary)

1 tablespoon cooking sake

1 tablespoon mirin

1 tablespoon sugar

2 whole nori sheets

2 cups Sushi Rice (page 17)

Japanese Egg Omelet (page 144), quartered lengthwise

1. In a saucepan, stir together the mushrooms, carrot, spinach, dashi powder, water, soy sauce, sake, mirin, and sugar. Bring to a boil over medium heat, reduce the heat to maintain a simmer, and cook for 15 minutes. Let it cool and drain.

2. Lay out the makisu on a work surface and place one sheet of nori on it, shiny-side down. Spread 1 cup of sushi rice evenly over the nori, leaving a 1-inch border visible.

CONTINUED

3. Lay half of the shiitake mushrooms below the middle of the rice. Place half of the carrot sticks, 5 stalks of the spinach, and 2 sticks of the omelet over the mushrooms. Fold back the ingredients that stick out from the side of the nori.

4. Begin rolling by picking up the edge of the makisu and nori closest to you and folding it over the ingredients. Hold the roll tightly to form a good shape. Let it sit, seam-side down, for 5 minutes at room temperature. Make another roll with the remaining nori, rice, and filling.

5. Cut each sushi roll into 8 pieces with a knife that is wiped on a clean, damp kitchen towel before each cut.

Spicy Tuna Roll

GLUTEN-FREE, NUT-FREE, PESCATARIAN

Makes 2 big rolls or 12 pieces

PREP TIME: 40 minutes

The spicy tuna roll is a novel creation and has become incredibly popular all over the world. But you won't find this roll in Japan. The key to making good-looking rice-side-out rolls is to place a piece of plastic wrap or parchment paper (about the same size as the makisu) on the rice and press lightly before flipping the roll over. This ensures that the rice and nori stick together nicely, which makes rolling and shaping easier.

2 whole nori sheets

2 cups Sushi Rice (page 17)

4 tablespoons roasted sesame seeds

1½ tablespoons Spicy Mayonnaise Sauce (page 147)

4 ounces sashimi-grade tuna, cut (see page 19)

1 baby cucumber, cut (see page 22)

1. Lay out the makisu on a work surface and place one piece of nori on it, shiny-side down. Spread 1 cup of sushi rice evenly over the nori. Sprinkle the rice with 2 tablespoons of sesame seeds.

2. Place a piece of plastic wrap or parchment paper (about the same size as the makisu) on the rice and flip so now the nori side is up.

CONTINUED

3. Spread about ½ tablespoon of the mayonnaise sauce in a line across the middle of the nori. Lay half of the tuna and 2 sticks of cucumber on the sauce.

4. Begin rolling by picking up the edge of the makisu and nori closest to you and folding it over the ingredients. Hold the roll tightly to form a good shape. Let it sit, seam-side down, for 2 minutes. Make three more rolls with the remaining nori, rice, sesame seeds, and filling.

5. Cut each sushi roll into 6 pieces with a knife that is wiped on a clean, damp kitchen towel before each cut. Transfer to a serving plate and put a little of the remaining ½ tablespoon of mayonnaise sauce on top of each piece.

California Roll

NUT-FREE,
PESCATARIAN

Makes 2 big
rolls or
12 pieces

PREP TIME:
25 minutes

This may be the first sushi roll ever created by a Japanese sushi chef in the United States. The key to making a great California roll, which has the rice side out, is to spread rice all over the nori without leaving any uncovered. In this recipe, 1 cup of sushi rice is used on one whole nori. This is the perfect amount for making tight sushi rolls that won't break apart.

2 whole nori sheets

2 cups Sushi Rice (page 17)

4 tablespoons roasted
sesame seeds

1 tablespoon mayonnaise

2 pieces leg-style imitation
crabmeat, cut (see page 22)

½ avocado, cut (see page 22)

1 baby cucumber, cut
(see page 22)

1. Lay out the makisu on a work surface and place one sheet of nori on it, shiny-side down. Spread 1 cup of sushi rice evenly over the nori. Sprinkle the rice with 2 tablespoons of sesame seeds. Place a piece of plastic wrap or parchment paper (about the same size as the makisu) on the rice and flip so the nori side is up.

2. Spread ½ tablespoon of mayonnaise in a line across the middle of the nori. On the mayonnaise, place 2 pieces of the imitation crabmeat and half of the avocado slices. Below the imitation crabmeat, place 2 sticks of cucumber.

3. Begin rolling by picking up the edge of the makisu and nori closest to you and folding it over the ingredients. Let it sit, seam-side down, for 5 minutes at room temperature. Make another roll with the remaining nori, rice, sesame seeds, and filling.

4. Cut each sushi roll into 6 pieces with a knife that is wiped on a clean, damp kitchen towel before each cut.

COOKING TIP: If it is hard to spread 1 cup of the rice on the nori, add the rice little by little until you barely see the nori.

Philadelphia Roll

GLUTEN-FREE,
NUT-FREE,
PESCATARIAN

Makes 4 thin
rolls or
24 pieces

PREP TIME:
40 minutes

Salmon and cream cheese is a very popular combination in Japan. These are great ingredients for appetizer dishes, such as summer rolls and sushi rolls. Roll and hold this sushi gently because it consists of only soft fillings, unlike other sushi rolls. Be careful not to press the roll too tight, because the cheese may squeeze out from the side. Also, when you cut the roll, use a sharp knife and pull the knife toward you carefully in one cut, so the filling stays inside.

2 whole nori sheets, halved

2 cups Sushi Rice (page 17)

4 tablespoons roasted sesame seeds

4 ounces sashimi-grade salmon, cut (see page 19)

¾ (8-ounce) package cream cheese, cut into ½-inch-thick sticks

2 teaspoons wasabi

Soy sauce (gluten-free if necessary)

1. Lay out the makisu on a work surface and place one piece of nori on it, shiny-side down. Spread ½ cup of sushi rice evenly over the nori. Sprinkle the rice with 1 tablespoon of sesame seeds.

2. Place a piece of plastic wrap or parchment paper (about the same size as the makisu) on the rice and flip so that the nori side is up.

3. Lay 3 pieces of the salmon across the middle of the nori, and arrange 1 or 2 pieces of the cream cheese sticks below the salmon.

4. Pick up the edge of the makisu and nori closest to you and roll it into a tight jelly roll. Let it sit, seam-side down, for 2 minutes. Make three more rolls with the remaining nori, rice, sesame seeds, and filling.

5. Cut each sushi roll into 6 pieces with a knife that is wiped on a clean, damp kitchen towel before each cut. Make the wasabi into a mound on the corner of a serving plate. Serve with a small, shallow dish of soy sauce for each person as needed.

Boston Roll

GLUTEN-FREE,
NUT-FREE,
PESCATARIAN

Makes 2 big
rolls or
12 pieces

PREP TIME:
35 minutes

COOK TIME:
5 minutes

If you want an eye-catching presentation, choose tail-on shrimp so the tail sticks out from the sushi roll. I recommend using deveined shrimp, but if you can't find them, devein them yourself by cutting a shallow slit on the back of the shrimp and removing the vein.

4 medium or large tail-on shrimp, deveined

2 whole nori sheets

2 cups Sushi Rice (page 17)

4 tablespoons roasted sesame seeds

½ avocado, cut (see page 22)

1 baby cucumber, cut (see page 22)

Soy sauce (gluten-free if necessary)

1. Fill a deep pan with water and bring it to a boil over high heat.

2. Meanwhile, carefully insert a skewer through the shrimp from head to tail to prevent them from curling when cooked. Place the skewer in the water and boil the shrimp over medium heat for 2 to 3 minutes until they turn pink. Once the shrimp are cool enough to handle, remove them from the skewer. Set aside.

3. Lay out the makisu on a work surface and place one sheet of nori on it, shiny-side down. Spread 1 cup of sushi rice evenly over the nori. Sprinkle the rice with 2 tablespoons of sesame seeds.

4. Place a piece of plastic wrap or parchment paper (about the same size as the makisu) on the rice and flip so that the nori side is up.

5. Lay 2 shrimp, tails sticking out of the nori, across the middle of the rice, and place half of the avocado and 2 sticks of cucumber below the shrimp.

6. Pick up the edge of the makisu and nori closest to you and fold it into a tight jelly roll. Make another roll with the remaining nori, rice, sesame seeds, and filling.

7. Cut each sushi roll into 6 pieces and serve with soy sauce.

Alaskan Roll

GLUTEN-FREE,
NUT-FREE,
PESCATARIAN

**Makes 2 big
rolls or
12 pieces**

PREP TIME:
30 minutes

COOK TIME:
1 minute

*This gorgeous roll is great for salmon lovers, with the perfect
marriage of the creamy, mild taste of salmon and the fresh
taste of asparagus. In this recipe, the asparagus is steamed in
the microwave to make it easier to prepare. It can be grilled or
panfried if you prefer.*

4 asparagus stalks, trimmed
and rinsed

2 whole nori sheets

2 cups Sushi Rice (page 17)

4 tablespoons roasted
sesame seeds

4 ounces sashimi-grade
salmon, cut (see page 19)

½ avocado, cut (see page 22)

1 teaspoon wasabi

2 tablespoons salmon roe

Soy sauce (gluten-free if
necessary)

1. On a microwave-safe plate, microwave the wet asparagus, covered, for about 40 seconds, until tender.

2. Lay out the makisu on a work surface and place one piece
of nori on it, shiny-side down. Spread 1 cup of sushi rice
evenly over the nori. Sprinkle the rice with 2 tablespoons of
sesame seeds.

3. Place a piece of plastic wrap or parchment paper (about
the same size as the makisu) on the rice and flip so the nori
side is up.

4. Lay 2 asparagus stalks across the middle of the nori. Arrange
half of the salmon and half of the avocado below the asparagus.

5. Pick up the edge of the makisu and nori closest to you and roll
it over the filling into a tight jelly roll. Let it sit, seam-side down,
for 5 minutes at room temperature. Make another roll with the
remaining nori, rice, sesame seeds, and filling.

6. Cut each sushi roll into 6 pieces, add a small wasabi mound on
the corner of a serving plate and ½ teaspoon of salmon roe on
each sushi piece, and serve with a small, shallow dish of soy
sauce for each person.

Mexican Roll

NUT-FREE,
PESCATARIAN

**Makes 2 big
rolls or
12 pieces**

*This roll topped with spicy pico de gallo will impress you with
its irresistible taste and texture. The key to making great,
crunchy tempura is to use cornstarch instead of flour. When
the tempura gets cold, flour tempura becomes soggy, but cornstarch tempura keeps its crunchiness. To make perfect, straight
shrimp tempura requires an extra step, which I will explain.*

PREP TIME:
35 minutes

COOK TIME:
5 minutes

4 medium or large tail-on
shrimp, peeled and deveined

1 tablespoon cornstarch

Vegetable oil, for frying

Tempura Batter (page 150)

2 whole nori sheets

2 cups Sushi Rice (page 17)

1 tablespoon Spicy
Mayonnaise Sauce (page 147)

½ avocado, cut (see page 22)

2 pieces leg-style imitation
crabmeat, cut (see page 22)
lengthwise

1 baby cucumber, cut (see
page 22)

½ cup Pico de Gallo (page 152)

1. Cut a vertical slice on the belly of the shrimp. Place the shrimp
   belly-side down on a cutting board and press the shrimp lightly
   against the board to break the tight muscles and straighten.
   Dredge the shrimp in the cornstarch.

2. In a deep pan, heat 2 inches of vegetable oil over medium heat
   until it shimmers. Dip the shrimp into the batter, then fry for
   2 minutes, flipping occasionally, until golden. Transfer to a wire
   rack to drain.

3. Put the makisu on a work surface. Place one sheet of nori on it,
   shiny-side down. Spread 1 cup of rice evenly over the nori. Place
   a piece of plastic wrap or parchment paper (about the same size
   as the makisu), on the rice, and flip so the nori side is up.

4. Spread ½ tablespoon of the mayonnaise sauce in a line across the middle of the nori, and lay 2 shrimp pieces (tails sticking out of the nori) on the sauce. Place half of the avocado, 2 pieces of the imitation crabmeat, and 2 sticks of cucumber below the shrimp.

5. Pick up the edge of the makisu and nori it into a tight jelly roll. Let it sit seam-side down for 5 minutes at room temperature. Make another roll with the remaining nori, rice, and filling.

6. Cut each sushi roll into 6 pieces and serve topped with pico de gallo.

COOKING TIP: To check whether the oil is hot enough to fry, drop in some batter. If it floats with bubbles, the oil is ready.

Rainbow Roll

NUT-FREE,
PESCATARIAN

Makes 2 big
rolls or
12 pieces

Rainbow rolls usually include many kinds of raw seafood and are covered with colorful ingredients. In this recipe, I use sliced avocado and sliced smoked salmon as the topping ingredients. When my sushi roll is misshapen, I cover the roll with avocado, sliced sashimi, or sliced cucumber as a topping to enhance the visual effect.

PREP TIME:
35 minutes

2 whole nori sheets

2 cups Sushi Rice (page 17)

4 ounces sashimi-grade tuna, cut (see page 19)

2 pieces leg-style imitation crabmeat, cut (see page 22)

1 baby cucumber, cut (see page 22)

4 ounces sliced smoked salmon

½ avocado, cut (see page 22)

1. Place the makisu on a work surface. Place one sheet of nori on it, shiny-side down. Spread 1 cup of sushi rice evenly over the nori. Put a piece of plastic wrap or parchment paper (about the same size as the makisu) on the rice and flip so the nori side is up.

2. Lay half of the tuna across the middle of the nori and arrange 2 pieces of imitation crabmeat and 2 sticks of cucumber below the tuna.

3. Pick up the edge of the makisu and nori into a tight jelly roll.

4. Remove the wrap and makisu, and place the roll seam-side down. Place half of the salmon and avocado slices diagonally next to each other over the roll. Cover the roll with the plastic wrap and hold tightly to make the salmon and avocado stick to the roll firmly. Let it sit for 5 minutes at room temperature. Make another roll with the remaining nori, rice, filling, and topping.

5. Cut each sushi roll into 6 pieces and serve.

COOKING TIP: Smoked salmon and avocado are easy to tear when you cut. To avoid that, cut the roll through the wrapper (if you use plastic wrap), so the topping keeps its shape.

Dragon Roll

GLUTEN-FREE,
NUT-FREE,
PESCATARIAN

Makes 2 big
rolls or
12 pieces

PREP TIME:
35 minutes

The Dragon Roll's appearance is reminiscent of dragon scales. To decorate this roll, overlap the edges of the sliced avocado repeatedly. If you can find cooked eel, top the roll with alternating slices of eel and avocado. In addition, this roll is sprinkled with agedama (tempura batter bits) to add a crunchy texture. You can also use store-bought agedama instead of homemade.

2 whole nori sheets

2 cups Sushi Rice (page 17)

4 ounces sashimi-grade tuna, cut (see page 19)

1 baby cucumber, cut (see page 22)

1 avocado, cut (see page 22)

Tempura Batter Bits (page 162)

Spicy Mayonnaise Sauce (page 147)

1. Put the makisu on a work surface. Place one sheet of nori on it, shiny-side down. Spread 1 cup of sushi rice evenly over the nori. Place a piece of plastic wrap or parchment paper (about the same size as the makisu) on the rice and flip so the nori side is up.

2. Arrange half of the tuna across the middle of the nori, and place 2 sticks of cucumber below the tuna.

3. Pick up the edge of the makisu and nori into a tight jelly roll. Remove the wrap and makisu, place the roll seam-side down, and arrange half of the avocado diagonally over the roll to mimic the pattern of dragon scales. Cover the roll with the wrap and hold tightly to make the avocado stick to the roll firmly. Let it sit for 5 minutes at room temperature. Make another roll with the remaining nori, rice, filling, and topping.

4. Cut each sushi roll into 6 pieces and serve with the batter bits sprinkled on top and a drizzle of the mayonnaise sauce.

SUBSTITUTION TIP: If you can get *tobiko* or *masago*, top each piece with about ¼ teaspoon of it instead of sprinkling with tempura batter bits.

Dynamite Roll

NUT-FREE,
PESCATARIAN

Makes 2 big
rolls or
12 pieces

PREP TIME:
40 minutes

COOK TIME:
5 minutes

Dynamite rolls usually consist of shrimp tempura and different kinds of vegetables. To create an impressive final presentation, choose tail-on shrimp so the tail sticks out from the end of the roll. Crispy fried onions add a great crunchy texture to the roll, and cucumber, sprouts, and red cabbage add color to the dish. You can use other vegetables, such as bell peppers, avocado, or celery, as additions or substitutions.

4 medium or large tail-on shrimp, deveined

1 tablespoon cornstarch

Vegetable oil, for frying

Tempura Batter (page 150)

2 whole nori sheets

2 cups Sushi Rice (page 17)

4 tablespoons roasted sesame seeds

2 tablespoons Spicy Mayonnaise Sauce (page 147), divided

1 baby cucumber, cut (see page 22)

½ cup bean sprouts, washed

½ cup shredded red cabbage

Sweet Eel Sauce (page 148)

½ cup store-bought crispy fried onions

1. Make small cuts vertically on the shrimp belly, place belly-side down on a cutting board, and press the shrimp lightly to straighten. Dredge the shrimp in the cornstarch.

2. In a deep pan, heat 2 inches of vegetable oil over medium heat until it shimmers. Dip the shrimp into the batter, then fry for 2 minutes, flipping occasionally, until golden. Transfer to a wire rack to drain.

3. Lay out the makisu on a work surface and place one sheet of nori on top, shiny-side down. Spread 1 cup of rice evenly over the nori, and sprinkle with 2 tablespoons of sesame seeds. Put a piece of plastic wrap or parchment paper (about the same size as the makisu) on the rice and flip so the nori side is up.

4. Spread about ½ tablespoon of the mayonnaise sauce across the middle of the nori. Place 2 shrimp, tails sticking out of the nori, on the sauce, and arrange 2 sticks of cucumber, ¼ cup of the sprouts, and ¼ cup of the cabbage below the shrimp.

5. Pick up the edge of the makisu and nori into a tight jelly roll. Let it sit, seam-side down, for 5 minutes at room temperature. Make another roll with the remaining nori, rice, sesame seeds, and filling.

6. Cut each sushi roll into 6 pieces and top each piece with a dash of the mayonnaise sauce, a drizzle of the eel sauce, and a sprinkle of fried onions.

Shellfish Roll

GLUTEN-FREE,
NUT-FREE,
PESCATARIAN

Makes 2 big rolls or 12 pieces

PREP TIME:
35 minutes

COOK TIME:
5 minutes

This is an incredibly delicious roll, and you should thank the sea for its blessing! If you prefer, you can make this a true treat by adding lobster. Cut the lobster into ½-inch-thick sticks and add it with the other ingredients.

4 medium or large shrimp, tail on, deveined

2 whole nori sheets

2 cups Sushi Rice (page 17)

4 tablespoons roasted sesame seeds

Wasabi

1 baby cucumber, cut (see page 22)

1 (4¼-ounce) can crabmeat, drained

6 sashimi-grade scallops, halved horizontally

2 tablespoons salmon roe

Soy sauce (gluten-free if necessary)

1. Fill a deep pan with water and bring it to a boil over high heat.

2. Skewer the shrimp from head to tail to prevent it from curling when cooked. Boil the shrimp over medium heat for 2 to 3 minutes, until it turns pink.

3. Put the makisu on a work surface and place one sheet of nori on it, shiny-side down. Spread 1 cup of rice evenly over the nori. Sprinkle the rice with 2 tablespoons of sesame seeds. Put a piece of plastic wrap or parchment paper (about the same size as the makisu) on the rice and flip so the nori side is up.

4. With your finger, spread a small amount of wasabi in a line across the middle of the nori. Place 2 shrimp pieces (tails sticking out of the nori) on the wasabi, and place 2 sticks of cucumber, 3 tablespoons of the crab, and 6 pieces of the scallop below the shrimp.

5. Pick up the edge of the makisu and nori closest to you, and roll into a tight jelly roll. Let it sit, seam-side down, for 5 minutes at room temperature. Make another roll with the remaining nori, rice, sesame seeds, and filling.

6. Cut each sushi roll into 6 pieces, top each piece with ½ teaspoon of the salmon roe, and serve with soy sauce.

Seared Bonito (Katsuo-no-Tataki) Roll

GLUTEN-FREE,
NUT-FREE,
PESCATARIAN

Makes 4 thin rolls or 24 pieces

PREP TIME:
40 minutes

This is a thin nori-side-out sushi roll filled with seared bonito, marinated sweet onion, and scallion. It seems like a traditional sushi roll, but Japanese tend to eat seared bonito as a sashimi dish. Even though seared bonito is categorized as sashimi, and the middle part is raw, it is eaten not with wasabi, but rather with grated ginger. Other common condiments for the bonito are garlic and Zingiber mioga (Japanese ginger).

2 whole nori sheets, halved

2 cups Sushi Rice (page 17)

4 ounces seared bonito, cut into ½-inch-thick and 2½-inch-long sticks

8 scallions, trimmed

½ cup Marinated Sweet Onion (page 137)

1 tablespoon peeled, grated fresh ginger

Ponzu Sauce (page 149)

1. Put the makisu on a work surface. Place one piece of nori on it, shiny-side down. Spread ½ cup of rice evenly over the nori, leaving a ½-inch border on the far side.

2. Place three pieces of the bonito and 2 scallions across the middle of the rice. Add 1 tablespoon of the onion on top.

3. Pick up the edge of the makisu and nori closest to you, attach the near edge of the rice to the far edge of the rice, and roll up. Let it sit, seam-side down, for a few minutes. Make three more rolls with the remaining ingredients.

4. Cut each sushi roll into 6 pieces and serve with a small mound of ginger and a dish of ponzu sauce.

Thai Shrimp Roll

GLUTEN-FREE,
PESCATARIAN

Makes 4 thin
rolls or
24 pieces

PREP TIME:
50 minutes

COOK TIME:
5 minutes

Thai food uses many vegetables, seafood, and lots of flavorful spices. If you like spicy Thai food, spread chili sauce on the nori before rolling it up. This is a thin roll, so I recommend using medium-size shrimp because it is hard to roll a large shrimp properly.

8 medium shrimp, deveined

2 whole nori sheets, halved

2 cups Sushi Rice (page 17)

½ cup bean sprouts, washed

8 cilantro sprigs, washed and trimmed

½ cup peanuts, crushed

Peanut Sauce (page 160)

1. Fill a deep pan with water and bring it to a boil over high heat.

2. Skewer the shrimp from head to tail to prevent it from curling when cooked. Boil the shrimp over medium heat for 2 to 3 minutes, until it turns pink.

3. Place the makisu on a work surface and place one piece of nori on it, shiny-side down. Spread ½ cup of rice evenly over the nori. Put a piece of plastic wrap or parchment paper (about the same size as the makisu) on the rice and flip so the nori side is up.

4. Place 2 shrimp across the middle of the nori and arrange one-quarter of the sprouts and 2 cilantro sprigs below the shrimp.

5. Pick up the edge of the makisu and nori it into a tight jelly roll. Let it sit, seam-side down, for a few minutes. Make three more rolls with the remaining nori, rice, and filling.

6. Cut each sushi roll into 6 pieces and serve sprinkled with peanuts and the peanut sauce drizzled on top.

Crab Salad Roll

GLUTEN-FREE,
NUT-FREE,
PESCATARIAN

Makes 4 thin
rolls or
24 pieces

PREP TIME:
45 minutes

Crabmeat dressed with mayonnaise goes really well with lettuce and sushi rice. There are a couple of substitutions you can use with this recipe: imitation crabmeat for real crabmeat, and regular mayonnaise for the wasabi mayonnaise sauce. In addition, lettuce can be used instead of nori. In that case, it is hard to keep a good sushi shape, so place the lettuce-wrapped sushi seam-side down on a plate.

1 (4¼-ounce) can crabmeat, drained

3 tablespoons mayonnaise

Salt

Freshly ground black pepper

2 whole nori sheets, halved

2 cups Sushi Rice (page 17)

4 tablespoons roasted sesame seeds

2 romaine lettuce leaves, halved lengthwise

Wasabi Mayonnaise Sauce (page 154)

1. In a small bowl, stir together the crabmeat and mayonnaise. Season with salt and pepper.

2. Put the makisu on a work surface and place one piece of nori on it, shiny-side down. Spread ½ cup of rice evenly over the nori. Sprinkle with 1 tablespoon of sesame seeds. Put a piece of plastic wrap or parchment paper (about the same size as the makisu) on the rice and flip so the nori side is up.

3. Place one piece of lettuce on the nori and place 2 tablespoons of the crabmeat mixture across the middle of the lettuce.

4. Pick up the edge of the makisu and nori into a tight jelly roll. Let it sit, seam-side down, for a few minutes. Make three more rolls with the remaining nori, rice, sesame seeds, and filling.

5. Cut each sushi roll into 6 pieces and drizzle with the mayonnaise sauce.

Cod Tempura Roll

GLUTEN-FREE,
NUT-FREE,
PESCATARIAN

Makes 4 thin
rolls or
24 pieces

PREP TIME:
40 minutes

COOK TIME:
20 minutes

Tempura is one of my favorite ways to eat cod. It has a soft texture and deliciously light taste. When you cut cod into sticks, cut carefully because it will easily crumble. In this recipe, the green beans are fried, just like the cod, but you can substitute sautéed, steamed, or boiled green beans for the tempura green beans.

1 (½ pound) cod fillet, cut into ½-inch-thick sticks

2 tablespoons cornstarch

Vegetable oil, for frying

Tempura Batter (page 150)

16 green beans, trimmed

2 whole nori sheets, halved

2 cups Sushi Rice (page 17)

Soy sauce (gluten-free if necessary)

1. Lay the cod on paper towels and blot dry. Dust the cod lightly with the cornstarch.

2. In a deep pan, heat 2 inches of vegetable oil over medium-low heat until it shimmers. Dip the cod into the batter, then fry for 4 minutes, flipping occasionally, until golden. Transfer to a wire rack to drain.

3. Dip the green beans into the batter, then fry for 2 to 3 minutes, flipping occasionally. Transfer to a wire rack to drain.

4. Put the makisu on a work surface. Place one piece of nori on it, shiny-side down. Spread ½ cup of sushi rice evenly over the nori, leaving a ½-inch border on the far side.

5. Across the middle of the rice, place one-quarter of the cod tempura and 4 green beans.

6. Pick up the edge of the makisu and nori closest to you, attach the near edge of rice to the far edge of the rice, and roll up. Let it sit, seam-side down, for a few minutes. Make three more rolls with the remaining nori, rice, and filling.

7. Cut each sushi roll into 6 pieces and serve with soy sauce.

Sweet Chili Shrimp Roll

Makes 4 thin
rolls or
24 pieces

PREP TIME:
50 minutes

COOK TIME:
5 minutes

Sweet chili sauce is a versatile sauce that can be easily transformed into other delicious sauces with a little ingenuity. A mixture of sweet chili, ketchup, and soy sauce is a great sauce for Chinese dishes, like sweet-and-sour pork. You can find sweet chili sauce at many Asian markets and on Amazon.

8 medium shrimp, deveined

2 whole nori sheets, halved

2 cups Sushi Rice (page 17)

4 tablespoons roasted sesame seeds

2 tablespoons sweet chili sauce

½ cup shredded red cabbage

½ cup bean sprouts, washed

Sweet Chili Mayonnaise Sauce (page 155)

1. Fill a deep pan with water and bring it to a boil over high heat.

2. Skewer the shrimp from head to tail to prevent it from curling when cooked. Boil the shrimp over medium heat for 2 to 3 minutes, or until it turns pink.

3. Put the makisu on a work surface and place one piece of nori on it, shiny-side down. Spread ½ cup of rice evenly over the nori and sprinkle 1 tablespoon of the sesame seeds on top. Put a piece of plastic wrap or parchment paper (about the same size as the makisu) on the rice and flip so the nori side is up.

4. Spread ½ tablespoon of chili sauce in a line across the middle of the nori. Place 2 shrimp on the sauce. Add one-quarter of the cabbage and one-quarter of the sprouts below the shrimp.

5. Pick up the edge of the makisu and nori into a tight jelly roll. Let it sit, seam-side down, for a few minutes. Make three more rolls with the remaining nori, rice, sesame seeds, and filling.

6. Cut each sushi roll into 6 pieces and drizzle with the chili mayonnaise.

Fried Shrimp Roll

NUT-FREE,
PESCATARIAN

**Makes 2 big
rolls or
12 pieces**

PREP TIME:
45 minutes

COOK TIME:
10 minutes

*This sushi has beautiful colors from the lettuce and egg and
a crunchy texture from the fried shrimp. This roll has an
eye-catching cross-section due to the layered shrimp, fried
egg, lettuce, nori, and rice. In Japan, both fried and tempura
shrimp are very popular and are frequently served as homemade dishes and at restaurants. The numerous steps may
seem excessive, but it's worth it. This sushi is delicious!*

1 teaspoon cornstarch

1 teaspoon water

2 eggs, beaten

Nonstick cooking spray

4 large tail-on shrimp,
deveined

2 tablespoons
all-purpose flour

½ cup bread crumbs

Vegetable oil, for frying

2 whole nori sheets

2 cups Sushi Rice (page 17)

1 romaine lettuce leaf, halved
lengthwise

Tempura Batter Bits (page 162)

Soy Sauce Mayonnaise Sauce
(page 156)

1. In a small dish, whisk together the cornstarch and water. Mix in
   the beaten egg.

2. Heat an 8-inch nonstick skillet over medium-high heat and
   coat with cooking spray. Pour half of the egg mixture into the
   skillet and spread to make a thin layer. Cook over low heat for
   3 minutes, flipping halfway through the cooking time. Make a
   second thin fried egg with the remaining egg mixture.

3. Make small cuts vertically on the shrimp belly, place belly-side
   down on a cutting board, and press the shrimp lightly to
   straighten. Bread the shrimp by coating them in the flour, then
   the egg, and then the bread crumbs.

4. In a deep pan, heat 2 inches of vegetable oil over medium heat until it shimmers. Fry the shrimp for 2 minutes, flipping occasionally, until golden. Transfer to a wire rack to drain.

5. Lay out the makisu on a work surface and place one sheet of nori on top, shiny-side down. Spread 1 cup of rice evenly over the nori. Put a piece of plastic wrap or parchment paper (about the same size as the makisu) on the rice and flip so the nori side is up.

6. Place a thin fried egg on the nori. Across the middle of the egg, place a piece of lettuce. On top of the lettuce place 2 shrimp, tails sticking out from the nori.

7. Pick up the edge of the makisu and nori into a tight jelly roll. Let it sit, seam-side down, for 5 minutes at room temperature. Make another roll with the remaining nori, rice, and filling.

8. Cut each sushi roll into 6 pieces, sprinkle with the tempura batter bits, drizzle with the mayonnaise sauce, and serve.

COOKING TIP: The cornstarch keeps the thin fried egg from tearing. However, if the egg cooks too long, it can shatter.

Buttery Scallop Roll

GLUTEN-FREE,
NUT-FREE,
PESCATARIAN

Makes 4 thin
rolls or
24 pieces

PREP TIME:
40 minutes

COOK TIME:
20 minutes

Buttery soy sauce with scallops is a favorite flavor of the Japanese. In this recipe, the scallop is halved to make it easier to cook all the way through. There are three ways to confirm that scallops are cooked through: by color (they should be golden brown on both sides), by texture (the scallop should break apart a little along the edge), and by consistency (with a touch of a finger, scallops come apart easily).

2 tablespoons butter or
margarine

12 scallops, halved horizontally

8 asparagus stalks, trimmed

2 tablespoons soy sauce
(gluten-free if necessary)

½ cup fresh corn kernels

2 whole nori sheets, halved

2 cups Sushi Rice (page 17)

4 tablespoons roasted
sesame seeds

1. In a skillet, melt 1 tablespoon of butter over medium heat. Add half the scallops and half the asparagus, and sauté for 5 minutes, flipping halfway through. Add 1 tablespoon of soy sauce and stir for 2 minutes. Transfer to a plate. Repeat with the remaining butter, scallops, asparagus, and soy sauce.

2. Add the corn to the empty skillet, and stir-fry over medium heat for about 5 minutes while scraping up the seasonings on the bottom of the skillet. Set aside.

3. Lay out the makisu on a work surface and place one piece of nori on it, shiny-side down. Spread ½ cup of rice evenly over the nori. Sprinkle with 1 tablespoon of the sesame seeds. Put a piece of plastic wrap or parchment paper (about the same size as the makisu) on the rice and flip so the nori side is up.

4. Lay 2 asparagus stalks across the middle of the nori, and arrange 6 scallop pieces on the asparagus.

5. Pick up the edge of the makisu and nori into a tight jelly roll. Let it sit, seam-side down, for a few minutes. Make three more rolls with the remaining nori, rice, sesame seeds, and filling.

6. Cut each sushi roll into 6 pieces, top each piece with 1 teaspoon of the corn, and serve.

Spicy Salmon Roll

GLUTEN-FREE,
NUT-FREE,
PESCATARIAN

Makes 4 thin
rolls or
24 pieces

PREP TIME:
45 minutes

The spicy tuna roll may be the most famous roll globally, but the popularity of the spicy salmon roll is catching up. Eating this spicy salmon roll is going to be an eye-opening experience for you. Sashimi salmon, spicy mayonnaise, and sharp-flavored arugula are put together in one roll. On top, the roll is covered with sliced cucumber and garnished with lemon zest that brings fresh taste and great balance.

2 whole nori sheets, halved

2 cups Sushi Rice (page 17)

2 tablespoons Spicy
Mayonnaise Sauce (page 147)

1 cup baby arugula

4 ounces sashimi-grade
salmon, cut (see page 19)

3 baby cucumbers, very thinly
sliced lengthwise

Zest of 1 lemon

1. Lay out the makisu on a work surface and place one piece of nori on it, shiny-side down. Spread ½ cup of rice evenly over the nori. Put a piece of plastic wrap or parchment paper (about the same size as the makisu) on the rice and flip so the nori side is up.

2. Spread ½ tablespoon of the sauce in a line across the middle of the nori. Spread one-quarter of the arugula on top of the sauce, and lay 3 pieces of the salmon on the arugula.

3. Pick up the edge of the makisu and nori into a tight jelly roll. Remove the wrap and makisu, place the roll seam-side down, and arrange the cucumber slices lengthwise on a slight diagonal over the roll. Cover the roll with the plastic wrap and hold tightly to make the cucumber stick to the roll firmly. Let it sit for a few minutes. Make three more rolls with the remaining nori, rice, and filling.

4. Cut each sushi roll into 6 pieces, sprinkle with lemon zest, and serve.

Fried Avocado Roll

NUT-FREE,
PESCATARIAN

Makes 2 big
rolls or
12 pieces

PREP TIME:
35 minutes

COOK TIME:
10 minutes

It seems that almost all sushi rolls around the world contain avocado. This roll contains fried avocado, sashimi tuna, and smoked salmon—a great combination of good fat and protein. The keys to cooking perfect fried avocado are to use avocado before it is ripe and to batter it properly. When the bread crumbs don't stick well to the avocado, dip the breaded avocado into the egg again and then press it into the bread crumbs.

1 avocado, cut lengthwise into
8 equal pieces

3 tablespoons
all-purpose flour

1 egg, beaten

¾ cup bread crumbs

Vegetable oil, for frying

2 whole nori sheets

2 cups Sushi Rice (page 17)

4 tablespoons roasted
sesame seeds

4 ounces sashimi-grade tuna,
cut (see page 19)

4 ounces sliced
smoked salmon

Sweet Eel Sauce (page 148)

1. Coat the avocado pieces in the flour, then the beaten egg, and then the bread crumbs.

2. In a deep pan, heat 2 inches of vegetable oil over medium heat until it shimmers. Add the avocado pieces and fry for 2 to 3 minutes, flipping occasionally, until golden. Transfer to a wire rack to drain.

3. Lay out the makisu on a work surface and place one sheet of nori on it, shiny-side down. Spread 1 cup of rice evenly over the nori. Sprinkle the rice with 2 tablespoons of sesame seeds. Put a piece of plastic wrap or parchment paper (about the same size as the makisu) on the rice and flip so the nori side is up.

4. Lay 4 pieces of the avocado across the middle of the nori, and arrange half of the tuna below the avocado.

5. Pick up the edge of the makisu and nori into a tight jelly roll. Remove the wrap and makisu, place the roll seam-side down, and arrange half of the smoked salmon slices next to each other lengthwise over the roll. Cover the roll with the plastic wrap and hold tightly to make the salmon stick to the roll firmly. Let it sit for 5 minutes at room temperature. Make another roll with the remaining nori, rice, sesame seeds, filling, and topping.

6. Cut each sushi roll into 6 pieces, drizzle with the sauce, and serve.

CLEANUP TIP: Do not drain the used oil down the sink. Instead, stuff paper towels into an empty can or jar for absorption, and pour the cooled oil into the container. Throw the can or jar into the regular garbage.

Negitoro Tempura Roll

GLUTEN-FREE,
NUT-FREE,
PESCATARIAN

Makes 4 thin
rolls or
24 pieces

PREP TIME:
50 minutes

COOK TIME:
10 minutes

When I first saw a fried sushi roll in my college cafeteria in the United States, I was so surprised and at a loss for words because I had never seen sushi cooked that way. It tasted great, so now I sometimes fry simple sushi rolls that contain one or two fillings. To make well-shaped fried rolls, hold the roll tightly as you're rolling. If the roll is loose, it can easily fall apart when it is dipped in the tempura batter.

4 ounces sashimi-grade tuna, finely minced

1 tablespoon soy sauce (gluten-free if necessary)

1 scallion, both white and green parts, chopped

2 whole nori sheets, halved

2 cups Sushi Rice (page 17)

Vegetable oil, for frying

Tempura Batter (page 150)

Tempura Dashi Sauce (page 151)

1. In a mixing bowl, stir together the tuna, soy sauce, and scallion.

2. Lay out the makisu on a work surface and place one piece of nori on it, shiny-side down. Spread ½ cup of rice evenly over the nori, leaving a ½-inch border on the far side.

3. Spread 2 tablespoons of the tuna mixture in a line across the middle of the rice.

4. Pick up the edge of the makisu and nori closest to you, attach the near edge of rice to the far side of the rice, and roll up. Let it sit, seam-side down, until the nori sticks firmly, for a few minutes. Make three more rolls with the remaining nori, rice, and filling.

5. In a deep pan, heat 2 inches of vegetable oil over medium heat until it shimmers. Dip the rolls in the batter, then fry until golden, about 2 to 3 minutes. Transfer to a wire rack to drain. Repeat with the remaining rolls.

6. Cut the sushi roll into 6 pieces and serve with a dish of dashi sauce.

Spicy Crab and Mango Roll

GLUTEN-FREE,
NUT-FREE,
PESCATARIAN

Makes 4 thin
rolls or
24 pieces

PREP TIME:
45 minutes

Mango brings out the flavor of seafood very well. If you haven't eaten these two things together, try this roll. It has a wonderful spicy and fresh taste with a touch of sweetness from the mango. You can use a 4¼-ounce can of lump crabmeat for this recipe if you prefer. Just be sure to drain before seasoning. You can also use imitation crab or any cooked seafood instead of crab.

4 ounces cooked crabmeat, coarsely chopped

1 teaspoon sweet chili sauce

Salt

Freshly ground black pepper

Juice of ½ lemon

2 whole nori sheets, halved

2 cups Sushi Rice (page 17)

½ avocado, cut (see page 22)

1 cup Spicy Mango Sauce (page 153)

1. In a bowl, stir together the crabmeat, the sweet chili sauce, a pinch of salt and pepper, and the lemon juice.

2. Lay out the makisu on a work surface and place one piece of nori on it, shiny-side down. Spread ½ cup of rice evenly over the nori. Put a piece of plastic wrap or parchment paper (about the same size as the makisu) on the rice and flip so the nori side is up.

3. Spread 2 tablespoons of the crab mixture in a line across the middle of the nori. Place 2 or 3 slices of avocado on top of the crab mixture.

4. Pick up the edge of the makisu and nori into a tight jelly roll. Make three more rolls with the remaining nori, rice, and filling.

5. Cut each sushi roll into 6 pieces, top with the mango sauce, and serve.

Salmon Teriyaki Roll

GLUTEN-FREE,
NUT-FREE,
PESCATARIAN

Makes 4 thin
rolls or
24 pieces

PREP TIME:
40 minutes

COOK TIME:
10 minutes

Do you struggle with cooking salmon all the way through? In this recipe I introduce you to seared sashimi salmon, where it doesn't matter if the inside of the salmon is uncooked. Salmon sashimi has an incredibly soft texture because of its high fat content. In comparison, tuna sashimi tends to get hard quickly when it's cooked. While you're cooking the salmon, treat it gently or it falls apart easily.

4 ounces sashimi-grade
salmon, cut (see page 19)

¼ cup Sweet Eel Sauce
(page 148)

2 whole nori sheets, halved

2 cups Sushi Rice (page 17)

4 tablespoons roasted
sesame seeds

8 parsley sprigs, trimmed

Wasabi Mayonnaise Sauce
(page 154)

4 scallions, both white and
green parts, chopped

1. In a dry nonstick skillet, cook the salmon over medium-low heat for 4 minutes, flipping occasionally. Add the eel sauce and cook for 2 minutes more, flipping frequently to coat the salmon.

2. Lay out the makisu and place one piece of nori on top, shiny-side down. Spread ½ cup of rice evenly over the nori. Spread 1 tablespoon of sesame seeds on the rice. Put a piece of plastic wrap or parchment paper (about the same size as the makisu) on the rice and flip so the nori side is up.

3. Arrange 3 pieces of salmon and 2 parsley sprigs across the middle of the nori.

4. Pick up the edge of the makisu and nori into a tight jelly roll. Let it sit, seam-side down, for a few minutes. Make three more rolls with the remaining nori, rice, sesame seeds, and filling.

5. Cut each sushi roll into 6 pieces, drizzle with the sauce, sprinkle with the scallions, and serve.

Egg Roll

GLUTEN-FREE,
NUT-FREE,
VEGETARIAN

Makes 3 thin rolls or 12 pieces

PREP TIME:
35 minutes

COOK TIME:
10 minutes

This is a very delicious and good-looking sushi roll wrapped with a thin layer of fried egg instead of nori. Because the egg wrapper has a round shape and the fried egg doesn't stick to any other ingredients, use less rice than you would in a regular thin roll and serve the cut sushi pieces seam-side down on a plate. Egg-wrapped sushi is very popular among my non-Japanese friends. It is a great recipe to master!

1 teaspoon cornstarch

1 teaspoon water

1 teaspoon soy sauce
(gluten-free if necessary)

2 eggs, beaten

Nonstick cooking spray

1 cup Sushi Rice (page 17)

1½ baby cucumbers, cut
(see page 22)

½ avocado, cut lengthwise into 6 equal pieces

1. In a small dish, whisk together the cornstarch and water. Mix in the soy sauce and the beaten eggs.

2. Heat an 8-inch nonstick skillet over medium-high heat and coat with cooking spray. Pour one-third of the egg mixture into the skillet and spread the egg over the surface of the skillet to make a thin layer. Cook over low heat for 3 minutes, flipping halfway through. Make two more thin fried eggs with the remaining egg mixture.

3. Lay out the makisu on a work surface and place one egg on top. Spread ⅓ cup of rice evenly over half the egg. Press the rice lightly.

4. Place 2 pieces of cucumber and 2 pieces of avocado on the rice.

5. Pick up the edge of the makisu and nori into a tight jelly roll. Let it sit, seam-side down, for a few minutes. Make two more rolls with the remaining eggs, rice, and filling.

6. Cut each sushi roll into 4 pieces and serve.

   COOKING TIP: Wrap the makisu with pieces of paper towel, parchment paper, or plastic wrap before placing the fried egg on top. This keeps the makisu from getting oil stains.

Zucchini Roll

NUT-FREE,
VEGETARIAN

Makes 4 thin
rolls or
24 pieces

PREP TIME:
50 minutes

COOK TIME:
15 minutes

With this recipe, I use black pepper for seasoning, but you can substitute sweet chili sauce if you prefer. The key to frying zucchini is to flour it well when breading it. If it is not coated well, the bread crumbs won't stick.

1 zucchini, cut into
½-inch-thick sticks

3 tablespoons
all-purpose flour

1 egg, beaten

¾ cup bread crumbs

Vegetable oil, for frying

2 whole nori sheets, halved

2 cups Sushi Rice (page 17)

¾ (8-ounce) package cream
cheese, cut into ½-inch-
thick sticks

1 avocado, cut (see page 22)

Freshly ground black pepper

1. Bread the zucchini by rolling it in the flour, then the egg, and then the bread crumbs.

2. In a deep pan, heat 2 inches of vegetable oil over medium heat until it shimmers. Fry the zucchini for 2 to 3 minutes, in batches if necessary, until golden. Transfer to a wire rack to drain.

3. Lay out the makisu on a work surface and place one piece of nori on top, shiny-side down. Spread ½ cup of rice evenly over the nori. Put a piece of plastic wrap or parchment paper (about the same size as the makisu) on the rice and flip so the nori side is up.

4. Arrange 2 or 3 pieces of the zucchini across the middle of the nori. Add 1 or 2 pieces of the cream cheese below the zucchini.

5. Pick up the edge of the makisu and nori into a tight jelly roll. Remove the wrap and makisu, place the roll seam-side down, and arrange one-quarter of the avocado slices next to one another lengthwise over the roll. Cover the roll with the plastic wrap and hold tightly to make the avocado stick to the roll firmly. Let it sit for 5 minutes at room temperature. Make three more rolls with the remaining nori, rice, filling, and topping.

6. Cut each sushi roll into 6 pieces, sprinkle with the black pepper, and serve.

Asparagus Roll

**Makes 4 thin
rolls or
24 pieces**

PREP TIME:
45 minutes

COOK TIME:
5 minutes

*This roll combines popular Japanese breakfast ingredients
into one roll. It has a great balance of nutrients from the egg,
asparagus, sesame seeds, and miso. This roll is a great dish
for parties because it is gluten-free, vegetarian, and delicious,
so most people can enjoy it. Frying is one of the best ways to
cook asparagus. It makes for a good, tender texture in a short
amount of time.*

Vegetable oil, for frying

8 asparagus stalks, trimmed
and washed

Tempura Batter (page 150)

2 whole nori sheets, halved

2 cups Sushi Rice (page 17)

4 tablespoons roasted
sesame seeds

Japanese Egg Omelet
(page 144), quartered
lengthwise and each quarter
halved crosswise

Miso Sesame Sauce (page 157)

1. In a deep pan, heat 2 inches of vegetable oil over medium-low
   heat until it shimmers. Dip the asparagus into the batter, then
   fry for 2 minutes, flipping occasionally, until golden. Transfer to
   a wire rack to drain.

2. Lay out the makisu on a work surface and place one piece of
   nori on top, shiny-side down. Spread ½ cup of rice evenly over
   the nori. Sprinkle 1 tablespoon of the sesame seeds over the
   rice. Place a piece of plastic wrap or parchment paper (about
   the same size as the makisu) on the rice and flip so the nori
   side is up.

3. Place 2 pieces of asparagus across the middle of the nori and
   arrange 1 or 2 omelet sticks below the asparagus.

4. Pick up the edge of the makisu and nori into a tight jelly roll. Let
   it sit, seam-side down, for 2 minutes. Make three more rolls with
   the remaining nori, rice, sesame seeds, and filling.

5. Cut each sushi roll into 6 pieces, drizzle the sauce on top,
   and serve.

Spicy Fried Mozzarella Roll

NUT-FREE,
VEGETARIAN

Makes 2 big rolls or 12 pieces

PREP TIME:
35 minutes

COOK TIME:
2 minutes

The main ingredient of this roll is fried mozzarella cheese sticks, which everybody loves. If you don't like spicy food, substitute ketchup for the pico de gallo and the spicy mayonnaise sauce. In fact, the combination of rice and ketchup is very popular in Japan. It is delicious!

3 mozzarella cheese sticks, halved

2 tablespoons all-purpose flour

1 egg, beaten

½ cup bread crumbs

Vegetable oil, for frying

2 whole nori sheets

2 cups Sushi Rice (page 17)

4 tablespoons roasted sesame seeds

1 romaine lettuce leaf, halved lengthwise

½ cup Pico de Gallo (page 152)

Spicy Mayonnaise Sauce (page 147)

1. Coat the mozzarella sticks in flour, then egg, and then bread crumbs.

2. In a deep pan, heat 2 inches of vegetable oil over medium heat until it shimmers. Fry the mozzarella, flipping occasionally, until golden, about 30 to 60 seconds. Transfer to a wire rack to drain.

3. Lay out the makisu on a work surface and place one piece of nori on top, shiny-side down. Spread 1 cup of sushi rice evenly over the nori. Spread 2 tablespoons of the sesame seeds on the rice. Put a piece of plastic wrap or parchment paper (about the same size as the makisu) on the rice and flip so the nori side is up.

4. Place a piece of lettuce across the middle of the nori. Place 3 pieces of the fried mozzarella on the lettuce, and spread ¼ cup of the pico de gallo in a line below the mozzarella.

5. Pick up the edge of the makisu and nori into a tight jelly roll. Let it sit for 5 minutes at room temperature. Make another roll with the remaining nori, rice, sesame seeds, and filling.

6. Cut each sushi roll into 6 pieces, drizzle with mayonnaise sauce, and serve.

Rainbow Veggie Roll

GLUTEN-FREE,
NUT-FREE,
VEGAN

Makes 2 big
rolls or
12 pieces

PREP TIME:
30 minutes,
plus
20 minutes
to marinate

COOK TIME:
5 minutes

This roll is a great lunch to eat on the go and becomes even easier on your schedule if you make it the night before. You can store this overnight in the refrigerator, but be sure to drizzle the avocado with juice from half a lemon so it does not turn brown.

1 tablespoon toasted
sesame oil

½ yellow bell pepper, sliced

½ cup Pickling Liquid
(page 161)

2 whole nori sheets

2 cups Sushi Rice (page 17)

4 tablespoons roasted
sesame seeds

1 romaine lettuce leaf, halved
lengthwise

1 baby cucumber, cut
(see page 22)

½ cup shredded red cabbage

1 avocado, cut (see page 22)

Finely ground Himalayan
pink salt

1. In a skillet, heat the sesame oil over medium heat until it shimmers. Add the bell pepper and cook for 5 minutes. In a bowl, stir together the bell pepper and the pickling liquid. Let it sit for 20 minutes at room temperature.

2. Lay out the makisu on a work surface and place one sheet of nori on top, shiny-side down. Spread 1 cup of sushi rice evenly over the nori. Sprinkle 2 tablespoons of the sesame seeds on top of the rice. Put a piece of plastic wrap or parchment paper (about the same size as the makisu) on the rice and flip so the nori side is up.

3. Lay a piece of the lettuce across the middle of the nori. Place 2 pieces of the cucumber, ¼ cup of the cabbage, and half of the pickled bell pepper on the lettuce.

4. Pick up the edge of the makisu and nori into a tight jelly roll. Remove the wrap and makisu, place the roll seam-side down, and arrange half of the avocado slices side by side lengthwise over the roll. Cover the roll with the wrap, and hold tightly to make the avocado stick to the roll firmly. Let it sit for 5 minutes at room temperature. Make another roll with the remaining nori, rice, sesame seeds, filling, and topping.

5. Cut each sushi roll into 6 pieces, sprinkle with salt, and serve.

Quinoa Salad Roll

**GLUTEN-FREE,
VEGAN**

**Makes 2 big
rolls or
12 pieces**

PREP TIME:
25 minutes

*This creative sushi roll uses quinoa instead of rice. Unlike rice,
cooked quinoa is not sticky, so make sure to press it well when
it is spread on the nori and to roll nori-side out. Using quinoa
has an advantage, as it doesn't dry out easily in the refrigerator
like sushi rice. Therefore, you can make this roll ahead of time
and keep it in the refrigerator, just like a quinoa salad!*

2 whole nori sheets

1 cup cooked quinoa

½ cup arugula

½ yellow bell pepper, sliced

1 medium tomato, seeded
and sliced

½ avocado, cut (see page 22)

Almond Sauce (page 159)

1. Lay out the makisu on a work surface and place one sheet of
   nori on it, shiny-side down. Spread ½ cup of the quinoa evenly
   over the nori, leaving a 2-inch border on the far side.

2. Place ¼ cup of arugula in a line across the middle of the quinoa.
   Place half of the bell pepper, half of the tomato, and half of the
   avocado on the arugula.

3. Pick up the edge of the makisu and nori into a jelly roll. Let it sit
   for 5 minutes at room temperature. Make another roll with the
   remaining nori, quinoa, and filling.

4. Cut each sushi roll into 6 pieces, drizzle with almond sauce,
   and serve.

Sweet Potato Tempura Roll

GLUTEN-FREE,
NUT-FREE,
VEGAN

Makes 2 big
rolls or
12 pieces

PREP TIME:
30 minutes

COOK TIME:
15 minutes

Sweet potato tempura has never been a main dish in Japan, but it is a very popular tempura ingredient. To make sure that the potato tempura is done, poke it with a toothpick, and when the toothpick slides easily all the way through, it is done. If not, fry for one more minute.

Vegetable oil, for frying

½ medium sweet potato, peeled and cut into ½-inch-thick sticks

Tempura Batter (page 150)

4 shiitake mushrooms, stemmed and halved

2 whole nori sheets

2 cups Sushi Rice (page 17)

4 tablespoons roasted sesame seeds

Tempura Dashi Sauce (page 151)

1. In a deep pan, heat 2 inches of vegetable oil over medium-low heat until it shimmers. Dip the sweet potato sticks into the batter, then fry about 4 pieces at a time for 3 minutes, flipping occasionally, until golden. Transfer to a wire rack to drain.

2. Dip the mushrooms into the batter, then fry for 1 to 2 minutes, flipping occasionally. Transfer to a wire rack to drain.

3. Lay out the makisu on a work surface and place one sheet of nori on top, shiny-side down. Spread 1 cup of sushi rice evenly over the nori. Sprinkle the rice with 2 tablespoons of the sesame seeds. Put a piece of plastic wrap or parchment paper (about the same size as the makisu) on the rice and flip so the nori side is up.

4. Arrange half of the sweet potato tempura in a line across the middle of the nori, and place 4 pieces of the shiitake mushrooms below the sweet potatoes.

5. Pick up the edge of the makisu and nori into a tight jelly roll. Let it sit, seam-side down, for 5 minutes at room temperature. Make another roll with the remaining nori, rice, sesame seeds, and filling.

6. Cut each sushi roll into 6 pieces and serve with a dish of dashi sauce.

Asparagus and Bacon Roll

GLUTEN-FREE, NUT-FREE

Makes 4 thin rolls or 24 pieces

PREP TIME: 40 minutes

COOK TIME: 20 minutes

Asparagus and bacon are made for each other. In this recipe, turkey bacon is used, but you can use any kind of bacon you like. Use soy bacon to make this roll vegetarian. Bacon is the perfect length for sushi rolls, so there is no need to cut. However, when you roll, you should fold the edge of the bacon back into the roll because the roll doesn't close when the bacon sticks out.

8 turkey bacon slices

8 asparagus stalks, trimmed

1 tablespoon butter or margarine

2 eggs, beaten

2 whole nori sheets, halved

2 cups Sushi Rice (page 17)

4 tablespoons roasted sesame seeds

1. In a dry nonstick skillet, cook the bacon. Transfer to a plate lined with paper towels to drain.

2. In the same skillet, cook the asparagus for 5 minutes, flipping occasionally, until softened slightly. Transfer to a plate.

3. In the skillet, melt the butter. Pour in the beaten egg and cook over medium heat for about 1 minute, moving a spatula across the bottom and sides of the skillet to make small curds. Remove from the heat and set aside.

4. Lay out the makisu on a work surface and place one piece of nori on it, shiny-side down. Spread ½ cup of rice evenly over the nori. Sprinkle the rice with 1 tablespoon of the sesame seeds. Put a piece of plastic wrap or parchment paper (about the same size as the makisu) on the rice and flip so the nori side is up.

5. Lay one piece of bacon across the middle of the nori. On top of the bacon, layer 2 asparagus stalks and another piece of bacon.

6. Pick up the edge of makisu and nori closest to you, and roll into a tight jelly roll. Let it sit, seam-side down, for 2 minutes. Make three more rolls with the remaining nori, rice, sesame seeds, and filling.

7. Cut each sushi roll into 6 pieces, top with the cooked egg, and serve.

Chicken Sausage Roll

GLUTEN-FREE, NUT-FREE, KID FRIENDLY

Makes 3 thin rolls or 12 pieces

PREP TIME: 30 minutes

COOK TIME: 15 minutes

This is the best sushi roll for kids—chicken sausage rolled with rice wrapped in a slightly sweet fried egg wrapper. You can substitute any kind of sausage you like. To fancy up this roll, serve with marinara sauce.

3 chicken sausages	2 eggs, beaten
1 teaspoon cornstarch	Nonstick cooking spray
1 teaspoon water	1 cup Sushi Rice (page 17)
1 teaspoon sugar	Ketchup

1. Cook the chicken sausages according to the package directions and set aside to cool.

2. In a small dish, whisk together the cornstarch and water. Mix in the sugar and the beaten eggs. Heat an 8-inch nonstick skillet over medium-high heat and coat with cooking spray. Pour one-third of the egg mixture into the skillet and spread the egg all over the surface of the skillet to make a thin layer. Cook over low heat for 3 minutes, gently flipping halfway through the cooking time with a rubber spatula. Make two more thin fried eggs with the remaining egg mixture.

3. Lay out the makisu on a work surface and place one piece of egg on top. Spread ⅓ cup of the rice evenly across half of the egg, and press the rice lightly.

4. Lay 1 sausage across the middle of the rice.

5. Pick up the edge of the makisu and nori into a tight jelly roll. Let it sit, seam-side down, for 2 minutes. Make two more rolls with the remaining egg, rice, and sausage.

6. Cut each sushi roll into 4 pieces, top with a dash of ketchup, and serve.

COOKING TIP: Wrap the makisu with pieces of paper towel, parchment paper, or plastic before placing the fried egg on top to keep the makisu from getting stained.

Chicken Katsu Roll

NUT-FREE

Makes 4 thin rolls or 24 pieces

PREP TIME:
45 minutes

COOK TIME:
10 minutes

Chicken katsu (fried chicken breast) is a staple dish in Japan. Katsu means "win" in Japanese, so sometimes people eat this before an exam or a game for good luck.

6 ounces chicken breast, cut into ½-inch-wide strips

Salt

Freshly ground black pepper

2 tablespoons all-purpose flour

1 egg, beaten

½ cup bread crumbs

Vegetable oil, for frying

2 whole nori sheets, halved

2 cups Sushi Rice (page 17)

4 tablespoons roasted sesame seeds

1 cup shredded cabbage

Sweet Eel Sauce (page 148)

1. Season the chicken with the salt and pepper.

2. Coat the chicken in the flour, then the egg, and then the bread crumbs.

3. In a deep pan, heat 2 inches of vegetable oil over medium heat until it shimmers. Fry the chicken for about 4 minutes, until golden, flipping occasionally. Transfer to a wire rack to drain.

4. Lay out the makisu on a work surface and place one piece of nori on top, shiny-side down. Spread ½ cup of rice evenly over the nori. Sprinkle with 1 tablespoon of sesame seeds. Place a piece of plastic wrap or parchment paper (about the same size as the makisu) on the rice and flip so the nori side is up.

5. Place one-quarter of the chicken across the middle of the nori, and place ¼ cup of the cabbage below the chicken.

6. Pick up the edge of the makisu and nori into a tight jelly roll. Let it sit, seam-side down, for a few minutes. Make three more rolls with the remaining nori, rice, sesame seeds, and filling.

7. Cut each sushi roll into 6 pieces, drizzle with the sauce, and serve.

SUBSTITUTION TIP: You can substitute lettuce for cabbage if you prefer.

Korean-Inspired Beef Roll

GLUTEN-FREE,
NUT-FREE

Makes 2 big
rolls or
12 pieces

PREP TIME:
25 minutes

COOK TIME:
10 minutes

This sushi roll has a delicious Korean flavor from the beef and seasoned sprouts. It is a very flavorful dish! In this recipe, the beef is seasoned with salt and black pepper and sautéed with minced garlic, but barbecue sauce can be used for seasoning if you prefer.

4 ounces sirloin steak, chuck steak, or rib eye steak, cut into ½-inch-thick strips

Pinch salt, plus 1 teaspoon

Freshly ground black pepper

1 tablespoon vegetable oil

2 garlic cloves, minced or grated, divided

1 cup bean sprouts, washed

1 tablespoon roasted sesame seeds

1 tablespoon toasted sesame oil

1 teaspoon soy sauce (gluten-free if necessary)

1 teaspoon sugar

2 whole nori sheets

2 cups Sushi Rice (page 17)

2 scallions, both white and green parts, chopped

Wasabi Mayonnaise Sauce (page 154)

1. Season the steak with a pinch of salt and black pepper. In a skillet, heat the oil and half of the garlic over medium heat, until the garlic starts browning. Cook the beef for 7 to 8 minutes, flipping occasionally, until it browns completely.

2. Microwave the sprouts for 60 to 90 seconds, until tender. Once they're cool enough to handle, squeeze excess water out by hand. In a bowl, stir together the sprouts, the other half of the garlic, sesame seeds, sesame oil, soy sauce, sugar, and 1 teaspoon of salt.

3. Lay out the makisu on a work surface and place one sheet of nori on top, shiny-side down. Spread 1 cup of rice evenly over the nori, leaving a 1-inch border on the far side of the nori.

4. Lay half of the steak across the middle of the rice. Arrange half of the sprouts below the beef.

5. Pick up the edge of the makisu and nori, attach the near edge of the rice to the rice on the far side, and roll up. Let it sit, seam-side down, for about 5 minutes at room temperature. Make another roll with the remaining nori, rice, and filling.

6. Cut each sushi roll into 6 pieces, sprinkle with scallions, drizzle with the mayonnaise sauce, and serve.

Taco Sushi Roll

GLUTEN-FREE,
NUT-FREE

Makes 2 big
rolls or
4 pieces

PREP TIME:
25 minutes

COOK TIME:
10 minutes

This roll includes traditional taco ingredients—meat, lettuce, cheese, and pico de gallo—wrapped just like a burrito. All of the ingredients are crumbled, so be sure to hold them properly with your fingers when you roll up. For the ground beef, it is best to choose 80 to 90 percent lean beef. If low-fat meat is used, the roll may have a dry texture.

1 tablespoon vegetable oil

4 ounces ground beef

½ teaspoon onion powder

½ teaspoon ground cumin

½ teaspoon chili powder

½ teaspoon garlic powder

½ tablespoon ketchup

Salt

Freshly ground black pepper

2 whole nori sheets

2 cups Sushi Rice (page 17)

½ cup shredded lettuce

½ cup Pico de Gallo (page 152)

½ cup shredded
cheddar cheese

1. In a skillet, heat the vegetable oil over medium heat until it shimmers. Add the beef and cook, breaking it up with a spatula, until it is browned and no longer pink, about 5 minutes. Drain the excess fat if any. Season with the onion powder, ground cumin, chili powder, garlic powder, ketchup, salt, and pepper. Cook, stirring, for 2 minutes.

2. Put the makisu on a work surface. Place one sheet of nori on it, shiny-side down, with the longer side closest to you. Using a wet rice paddle, spread 1 cup of sushi rice evenly over the nori. Leave a 1-inch border on the far side of the nori.

3. Arrange ¼ cup of the beef in a line across the middle of the rice, and lay ¼ cup of the lettuce, ¼ cup of pico de gallo, and ¼ cup of the cheese below the beef.

4. Pick up the edge of the makisu and nori closest to you, and keep the filling in place with your fingers. Attach the near edge of the rice to the far edge of the rice and roll up. Hold the roll tightly to form a good shape. Let it sit, seam-side down, for about 5 minutes at room temperature. Make another roll with the remaining nori, rice, and filling.

5. Wrap the roll with a piece of parchment paper. To serve, halve crosswise at an angle.

SUBSTITUTION TIP: You can add avocado or guacamole to the roll as a filling. In that case, reduce the other filling ingredients by half, so the roll will close well.

Sweet-and-Sour Pork Roll

GLUTEN-FREE,
NUT-FREE

Makes 2 big
rolls or
12 pieces

PREP TIME:
25 minutes

COOK TIME:
5 minutes

The Chinese dish sweet-and-sour pork is a very popular home-made food in Japan. The fruity pineapple tastes great in a roll! In fact, pineapple contains enzymes that break up proteins, which allows our bodies to digest the meat better. It is important for optimal health benefits that the pineapple not be cooked over 140°F. I use Spam to make this recipe easier and tastier. When you bite into this roll, you will be hit with delicious flavors.

1 tablespoon vegetable oil

½ (12-ounce) can Spam, diced

¼ onion, sliced

¼ cup Sweet-and-Sour Sauce (page 158), plus more for dressing the roll

2 whole nori sheets

2 cups Sushi Rice (page 17)

½ cup chopped pineapple

2 scallions, both white and green parts, chopped

1. In a skillet, heat the vegetable oil over medium heat until it shimmers. Add the Spam and the onion, and cook for 3 minutes. Add the sweet-and-sour sauce and stir-fry for 2 minutes, until the Spam and onion are well coated, then remove from the heat.

2. Lay out the makisu on a work surface and place one sheet of nori on top, shiny-side down. Spread 1 cup of rice evenly over the nori. Put a piece of plastic wrap or parchment paper (about the same size as the makisu) on the rice and flip so the nori side is up.

3. Place half of the cooked meat mixture in a line across the middle of the nori, and lay ¼ cup of the pineapple below the meat.

4. Pick up the edge of the makisu and nori into a tight jelly roll. Let it sit, seam-side down, for about 5 minutes at room temperature. Make another roll with the remaining nori, rice, and filling.

5. Cut each sushi roll into 6 pieces, sprinkle with the scallions, drizzle with the sauce, and serve.

Ginger Chicken Roll

GLUTEN-FREE,
NUT-FREE

**Makes 2 big
rolls or
12 pieces**

PREP TIME:
30 minutes,
plus
15 minutes
to marinate

COOK TIME:
10 minutes

This is typical homemade Japanese food. It is an incredibly delicious and flavorful dish. Pork is usually used in the traditional recipe, but I use chicken thigh because it is delicious and stays tender after getting cold. The cooked ginger chicken can be stored in the refrigerator for up to 4 days, so you can make it ahead of time and just microwave with a cover for about 30 seconds when you're ready to make the roll.

6 ounces boneless, skinless chicken thighs, cut into ½-inch-wide strips

2 teaspoons peeled, grated fresh ginger

2 tablespoons soy sauce (gluten-free if necessary)

2 tablespoons cooking sake

1 tablespoon mirin

1 tablespoon toasted sesame oil

2 whole nori sheets

2 cups Sushi Rice (page 17)

4 tablespoons roasted sesame seeds

¼ onion, thinly sliced

½ cup shredded red cabbage

2 scallions, both white and green parts, chopped

Mayonnaise

1. In a large bowl, combine the chicken, ginger, soy sauce, cooking sake, and mirin. Stir until the chicken is coated. Refrigerate to marinate for at least 15 minutes.

2. In a skillet, heat the sesame oil over medium heat until it shimmers. Add the chicken with the marinade and cook for 7 minutes, stirring continuously, until the chicken is cooked through.

3. Lay out the makisu on a work surface and place one sheet of nori on top, shiny-side down. Spread 1 cup of rice evenly over the nori. Sprinkle 2 tablespoons of sesame seeds on top. Put a piece of plastic wrap or parchment paper (about the same size as the makisu) on the rice and flip so the nori side is up.

4. Place half of the chicken in a line across the middle of the nori, and lay half of the onion and ¼ cup of the red cabbage below the chicken.

5. Pick up the edge of the makisu and nori into a tight jelly roll. Let it sit, seam-side down, for about 5 minutes at room temperature. Make another roll with the remaining nori, rice, sesame seeds, and filling.

6. Cut each sushi roll into 6 pieces, sprinkle with the scallions, drizzle with the mayonnaise, and serve.

BLT Roll

GLUTEN-FREE,
NUT-FREE

Makes 3 thin
rolls or
12 pieces

PREP TIME:
30 minutes

COOK TIME:
15 minutes

This creative Western sushi roll makes it hard to believe that you are eating sushi when you bite into it! Bacon, lettuce, and tomato go really well not only with white bread but also with sushi rice! To keep the roll from getting soggy, remove the tomato seeds to lower the moisture from the tomato.

1 teaspoon cornstarch

1 teaspoon water

1 teaspoon sugar

2 eggs, beaten

Nonstick cooking spray

3 turkey bacon slices

1 cup Sushi Rice (page 17)

1 large lettuce leaf, cut into 3 equal pieces

1½ tablespoons mayonnaise

1 small tomato, seeded and sliced

1. In a small bowl, whisk together the cornstarch and water. Mix in the sugar and the eggs.

2. Heat an 8-inch nonstick skillet over medium-high heat and coat with cooking spray. Pour one-third of the egg mixture into the skillet and spread the egg over the surface of the skillet to make a thin layer. Cook over low heat for 3 minutes, flipping halfway through the cooking time. Make two more thin fried eggs with the remaining egg mixture.

3. In a dry nonstick skillet, cook the bacon over medium heat for 5 minutes, flipping occasionally.

4. Lay out the makisu on a work surface and place one piece of egg on top. Spread ⅓ cup of rice over half of the egg and press the rice lightly.

5. Add 1 piece of lettuce across the middle of the rice. Spread ½ tablespoon of mayonnaise in a line on the lettuce, place 1 bacon slice on the mayo, and arrange one-third of the tomato on the bacon.

6. Pick up the edge of the makisu and nori into a tight jelly roll. Let it sit, seam-side down, for a few minutes. Make two more rolls with the remaining ingredients.

7. Cut each sushi roll into 4 pieces and serve.

Traditional
Big Roll
(Futomaki),
page 70

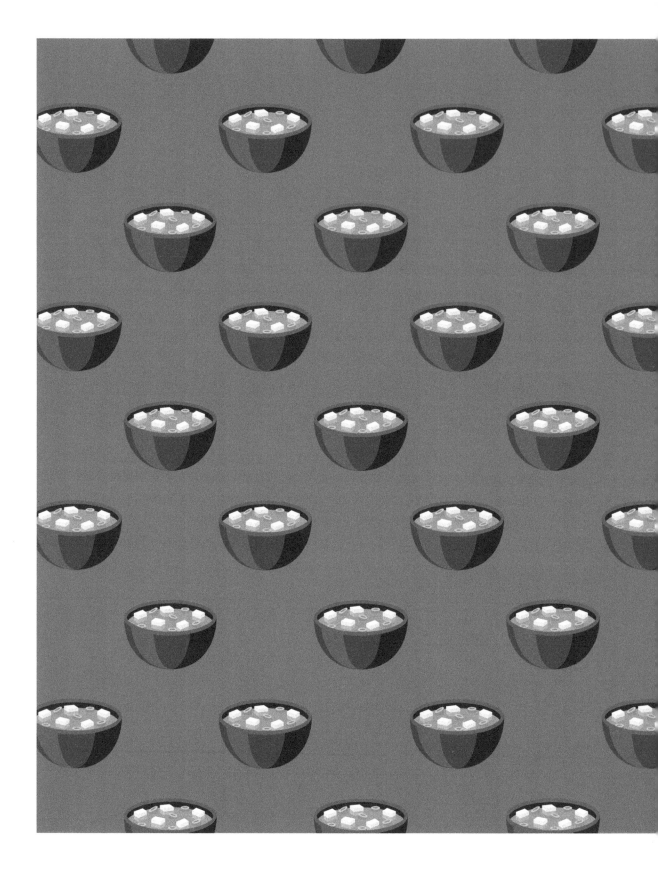

CHAPTER

5

Soups, Side Dishes, and Drinks

IN THIS CHAPTER, WE WILL EXPLORE SOUP AND SIDE DISH recipes and also learn about the tea and sake that are traditionally served in most Japanese sushi restaurants. These recipes and drinks go exceptionally well with sushi, as a matter of both taste and nutrition. Please remember that Japanese soup and side dishes are served in small quantities, so each recipe in this chapter includes the serving sizes in line with traditional Japanese custom. The recipes are very easy and will be a hit when you serve them with your homemade sushi!

Clockwise from the top: Japanese Sake (Nihon-Shu), page 141; Tofu and Seaweed Miso Soup, page 127; Cucumber and Ginger Pickles, page 133

Tofu and Seaweed Miso Soup

GLUTEN-FREE,
NUT-FREE,
VEGAN

Serves 4

PREP TIME:
25 minutes

COOK TIME:
10 minutes

Miso soup is an important dish in Japanese cuisine. Miso (soybean paste) is a traditional fermented food that is full of nutrition and is thought to keep the doctor away. In fact, there have been many studies that show the good effects of miso on human health. Miso loses many of its positive health benefits when it is cooked over high heat, so turn off the heat once the miso is dissolved. Miso contains small pieces of soybeans, so use a fine-mesh strainer when dissolving.

2 tablespoons dried wakame seaweed

5 cups water, divided

½ (14-ounce) package soft or firm tofu

2 teaspoons Shimaya kombu dashi soup stock powder, or any vegetable-based dashi powder

3 tablespoons mixed miso paste (*awase*)

1. In a bowl, stir together the wakame and 2 cups of water. Let it reconstitute for 10 minutes at room temperature. Drain.

2. Drain the tofu, wrap in paper towels, and microwave for 90 seconds. Let sit for 10 minutes to drain completely. Cut into 1-inch cubes.

3. Fill a saucepan with 3 cups of water and add the dashi powder. Bring to a boil over medium heat, add the wakame and the tofu, let the mixture resume boiling, reduce the heat to low, and simmer for 2 minutes.

4. Set a 5-inch fine-mesh hand strainer in the pan. Place the miso paste in the strainer. Using a spoon, dissolve the miso in the soup. Turn off the heat. Serve in miso soup bowls or small soup bowls.

SUBSTITUTION TIP: When you use soft tofu, skip the tofu-draining process. And treat it with extra care because it breaks easily.

INGREDIENT TIP: Dried wakame is a very handy ingredient to make any dish healthier. Just reconstitute for about 10 minutes and add it to salad, soup, or sautéed dishes.

Clam Miso Soup

GLUTEN-FREE,
NUT-FREE,
PESCATARIAN

Serves 4

PREP TIME:
5 minutes

COOK TIME:
10 minutes

Clam miso soup is very easy to make and incredibly flavorful. Clams have a lot of umami flavor, so there is no need to add dashi soup stock. Canned clams or frozen clams can also be used for this recipe if doing so is handier. If the clams are frozen, thaw first according to the package directions and add to the boiling water. Red miso is used in this recipe, and it can be found at most Asian markets or on Amazon.

3 cups water

⅓ cup canned clams

3 tablespoons red miso paste (also called *aka*)

2 scallions, both white and green parts, chopped

1. In a saucepan, boil the water over medium heat, add the clams, bring back to a boil, then reduce the heat to low, and simmer for 2 minutes.

2. Set a 5-inch fine-mesh hand strainer in the pan. Using a spoon, place the miso paste in the strainer and dissolve in the soup, stirring occasionally. Turn off the heat and add the scallions to the pan. Serve in miso soup bowls or small soup bowls.

SUBSTITUTION TIP: If you use shell-on clams, the soup becomes more flavorful! Prepare 5 clams per serving. Stir water (make sure the clams are not completely covered), salt (½ tablespoon per 1 cup water), and clams together in a bowl. Cover with a kitchen towel to make completely dark, and let sit at room temperature for 1 hour. Wash the clams under running water while stirring with your hand. Add the clams to a pan of boiling water, as in step 1 of this recipe. When the shells open, it means they are cooked through. (To ensure that the clams are safe to eat, do not eat any that aren't closed before cooking and that don't open after cooking.)

Carrot and Spinach Clear Dashi Soup (Sumashi-Jiru)

GLUTEN-FREE,
NUT-FREE,
VEGAN

Serves 4

PREP TIME:
5 minutes

COOK TIME:
15 minutes

Japanese eat clear dashi soup as often as miso soup. You can add any ingredients to this soup to change it up. Try daikon radish, napa cabbage, tofu, and mushrooms. Traditional Japanese soup has only a small number of ingredients so that you can enjoy tasting the flavorful dashi soup. Therefore, it is important to make sure you don't add too many ingredients and that the ingredients you add don't have a strong flavor.

3 cups water

2 teaspoons Shimaya kombu dashi soup stock powder, or any vegetable-based dashi powder

1 small carrot, peeled and thinly sliced

3 tablespoons cooking sake

1½ tablespoons soy sauce (gluten-free if necessary)

¼ teaspoon salt

20 spinach stalks, washed, trimmed, and cut into 2-inch lengths

In a saucepan, stir together the water, dashi powder, and carrot. Bring it to a boil over medium heat, for about 5 minutes. Reduce the heat to low, stir in the cooking sake, soy sauce, and salt, and simmer for 5 minutes. Add the spinach to the pan and cook for about 2 minutes, until tender. Serve in miso soup bowls or small soup bowls.

Egg Drop Soup

GLUTEN-FREE,
NUT-FREE,
VEGETARIAN

Serves 4

PREP TIME:
5 minutes

COOK TIME:
5 minutes

To cook great egg drop soup, boil the soup completely before and while pouring the egg so that the egg becomes curd. If the soup is not hot enough, the eggs take a longer time to curd, which may make them stick to the bottom of the pan. After pouring the eggs, be sure to turn the heat to low immediately and then simmer with a lid. Timing is important so you should pour the eggs slowly but expeditiously.

2 eggs, beaten

½ teaspoon salt

3 cups water

2 teaspoons Shimaya kombu dashi soup stock powder, or any vegetable-based dashi powder

1 scallion, both white and green parts, chopped

1. Whisk together the eggs and salt. Set aside.

2. In a saucepan, stir together the water and dashi powder, and bring to a boil over medium-high heat.

3. Pour the egg mixture slowly into the pan over chopsticks or fork tines, little by little. When all of the mixture is poured, immediately reduce the heat to low, and let it sit for 2 minutes with a lid on.

4. Stir gently, pour into small serving bowls, and sprinkle each serving with one-quarter of the scallion.

COOKING TIP: Pour the egg in batches, little by little, so you don't need to stir the soup while pouring the egg.

SUBSTITUTION TIP: If you want to cook Western-tasting egg drop soup, you can use consommé soup stock. It is also delicious!

Udon Noodle Soup

NUT-FREE, PESCATARIAN

Serves 6

PREP TIME:
5 minutes

COOK TIME:
15 minutes

Udon noodle soup is also a popular choice for the last course of a sushi meal. This dish is very simple. It includes udon noodles, a delicious fish dashi broth, and scallions. Udon noodle soup is comfort food for Japanese people, and it has a role similar to chicken noodle soup for Americans. Japanese people often eat this soup when we don't have any appetite or when we are sick. Use dried udon noodles for this recipe, as they are easy to get from the international aisle in most grocery stores or on Amazon.

1 (9.5-ounce) package Hakubaku organic udon noodles

6 cups water

1 tablespoon Ajinomoto Hondashi bonito soup stock powder, or any dashi powder you like

2 tablespoons soy sauce

1 tablespoon cooking sake

1 teaspoon salt

3 scallions, chopped

1. Bring a large stockpot of water to a boil over high heat. Cook the noodles according to the package directions. Drain and rinse the noodles under cool running water to stop the cooking process. Set aside.

2. In a saucepan, stir together the water, the stock base, soy sauce, cooking sake, and salt, and bring to a boil over medium-high heat.

3. Divide the cooked noodles into six portions and transfer each portion to a deep serving bowl. Pour 1 cup of the soup over the noodles in each bowl, and sprinkle with the scallions.

Cucumber, Wakame, and Imitation Crabmeat Sunomono

NUT-FREE,
PESCATARIAN

Serves 4

PREP TIME:
15 minutes

This is a very healthy, delicious, and light-tasting side dish (sunomono means "cold side dish"). The ingredients are prepared by salting or boiling, and though this may seem like a salad, it is not categorized as one in Japanese cuisine. Wakame seaweed is high in soluble fiber and aids in food digestion. Overall, this tasty side dish goes really well with sushi dishes!

2 tablespoons dried wakame seaweed

2 cups water

2 baby cucumbers, trimmed and thinly sliced crosswise

½ teaspoon salt

3 pieces leg-style imitation crabmeat, sliced lengthwise

2 tablespoons rice vinegar

1 teaspoon soy sauce (gluten-free if necessary)

1 teaspoon sugar

1 teaspoon cooking sake

1 teaspoon roasted sesame seeds

1. In a bowl, stir together the wakame and 2 cups of water, and let it reconstitute for 10 minutes at room temperature. Drain and wring it dry by hand.

2. Meanwhile, in a small bowl, combine the cucumbers and salt. Let them sit for 5 minutes at room temperature. Rinse the cucumbers under running water and wring them dry by hand.

3. In a mixing bowl, stir together the wakame, cucumbers, imitation crabmeat, rice vinegar, soy sauce, sugar, cooking sake, and sesame seeds. Divide among serving bowls and serve.

Cucumber and Ginger Pickles

GLUTEN-FREE,
NUT-FREE,
VEGAN

Serves 4

PREP TIME:
10 minutes,
plus 1 hour
to marinate

The delicious flavors of ginger and sesame oil dress the cucumber beautifully. The key to marinating cucumber in a short amount of time is to break the cucumber with a rolling pin so the resulting irregular surface is easily coated by the marinade. Fresh ginger has amazing health benefits, such as helping blood flow, increasing metabolism, and blocking the oxidation process in our bodies. You can use any kind of cucumber you prefer, but I recommend baby cucumbers, because they contain less water.

3 baby cucumbers

2 tablespoons toasted sesame oil

1 tablespoon soy sauce (gluten-free if necessary)

1 tablespoon rice vinegar

1 teaspoon peeled, grated fresh ginger

¼ teaspoon salt

2 teaspoons roasted sesame seeds

1. Wrap each cucumber with a kitchen towel and smash it with a rolling pin until it breaks into ½- to 1-inch pieces. Use your fingers to adjust the pieces to the correct size.

2. In a medium bowl, stir together the sesame oil, soy sauce, rice vinegar, ginger, and salt. Add the cucumber and mix well. Cover and marinate for at least 1 hour in the refrigerator. Sprinkle with sesame seeds and transfer to a small dish for each person.

STORAGE TIP: Transfer the pickles to a clean container with a cover. Store for up to 3 days in the refrigerator.

Agedashi Tofu

Serves 4

PREP TIME:
10 minutes

COOK TIME:
30 minutes

Agedashi tofu is one of the most popular dishes in Japanese restaurants in the United States. Ordinarily, the tofu is floured and deep-fried for this recipe. However, for homemade cooking, I think deep-frying is a little bit too much work when it is not necessary to make a dish delicious. Here, I will introduce you to an easy and healthy version of agedashi tofu using a small amount of oil for frying.

1 (14-ounce) package firm tofu

2 cups water

1 teaspoon Shimaya kombu dashi soup stock powder, or any vegetable-based dashi powder

2 tablespoons soy sauce (gluten-free if necessary)

2 tablespoons cooking sake

2 tablespoons mirin

½ cup cornstarch

4 tablespoons vegetable oil

1 scallion, chopped

2 teaspoons peeled, grated fresh ginger

1. Drain the tofu and wrap it in paper towels, then put it on a microwave-safe plate. Microwave for 3 minutes. Change the paper towels if they are completely soaked, then put a weight (such as a heavy plate) on the wrapped tofu for at least 10 minutes to drain completely.

2. Meanwhile, in a saucepan, stir together the water, dashi powder, soy sauce, cooking sake, and mirin, and bring to a boil over medium-high heat.

3. Cut the tofu into 2-by-2-inch squares about 1 inch thick. Put the cornstarch in a shallow bowl. Dredge the tofu in the cornstarch and tap off any excess.

4. In a nonstick skillet, heat 2 tablespoons of vegetable oil over medium heat until it shimmers. Add half of the coated tofu and cook for approximately 12 minutes, flipping halfway through the cooking time, until golden on both sides. Transfer to a wire rack to drain. Repeat with the remaining vegetable oil and tofu.

5. Divide the tofu among four serving plates. Drizzle each portion with the sauce, sprinkle with the scallion, and top with ½ teaspoon of the ginger.

Japanese Mountain Yam (Naga-Imo) and Sashimi Tuna

GLUTEN-FREE,
NUT-FREE,
PESCATARIAN

Serves 4

PREP TIME:
10 minutes

Naga-imo *is a somewhat rare potato that can be eaten raw. It has a beige color and thin hairy skin, and has a very light taste and a crisp texture. Naga-imo is rich in diastase, a digestive enzyme that helps digestion and absorption of nutrients into the body. It contains calcium oxalate, so it can sometimes make your hands or lips feel itchy when you touch it, but the itching will stop if you apply vinegar and warm water.*

½ pound sashimi-grade tuna, cut into ½-inch cubes

1 (6-ounce) Japanese mountain yam, peeled and cut into ½-inch dice

2 tablespoons soy sauce (gluten-free if necessary)

2 tablespoons rice vinegar

1 teaspoon mirin

Wasabi

1. In a bowl, stir together the tuna, yam, soy sauce, rice vinegar, and mirin.

2. Divide the mixture among four small dishes and top with a dash of wasabi.

GROCERY TIP: You can find naga-imo at most Asian markets and some grocery stores. In grocery stores, it might be labeled "naga-imo," "mountain yam," or "Chinese yam."

Japanese-Style Oven-Fried Chicken

GLUTEN-FREE,
NUT-FREE

Serves 4

PREP TIME:
10 minutes,
plus
15 minutes
to marinate

COOK TIME:
20 minutes

This is an essential main dish in Japan, called karaage. *Nowadays, the dish is popular as a side dish in sushi restaurants. The chicken is marinated in delicious sauce, which is a mixture of soy sauce, garlic, ginger, and cooking sake. The chicken is fried in the oven so you can enjoy flavorful, tender, and juicy fried chicken without using large quantities of hot oil.*

Nonstick cooking spray

3 pounds boneless, skinless chicken thighs (6 to 8 thighs), cut into 2-inch pieces

4 tablespoons soy sauce (gluten-free if necessary)

2 tablespoons cooking sake

2 teaspoons peeled, grated fresh ginger

2 teaspoons grated garlic

$2/3$ cup cornstarch

3 tablespoons vegetable oil

1. Preheat the oven to 400°F. Coat a foil-lined, rimmed baking sheet with cooking spray and set aside.

2. In a large bowl, combine the chicken, soy sauce, cooking sake, ginger, and garlic. Ensure the chicken is covered by the sauce, and refrigerate to marinate for 15 minutes.

3. Put the cornstarch in a shallow bowl. Dredge the chicken in the cornstarch and tap off any excess.

4. Place the chicken on the prepared baking sheet. Brush the chicken lightly with the vegetable oil.

5. Bake for 20 minutes until browned. Let the chicken sit for about 5 minutes on the range to cool.

Marinated Sweet Onion

GLUTEN-FREE,
NUT-FREE,
PESCATARIAN

Serves 4

PREP TIME:
10 minutes,
plus 1 hour
to marinate

Onions contain high amounts of vitamin B_6 and potassium, which are both good for health. Onion that's been immersed in water has a less pungent taste than fresh onion. Onions contain allyl sulfide, which is soluble in water, so as it seeps into the water, the pungent taste is reduced. But soaking may cause other good elements, such as potassium and vitamin B, to soak out, so it is preferable to soak the onion in water for a maximum of 5 minutes.

½ sweet or yellow onion, thinly sliced

2 tablespoons extra-virgin olive oil

1 tablespoon rice vinegar

1 teaspoon sugar

½ teaspoon salt

Freshly ground black pepper

Roasted sesame seeds, for topping

1. In a small bowl, soak the onion for 5 minutes in enough water to cover. Drain and wring out by hand.

2. In another small bowl, stir together the onion, olive oil, rice vinegar, sugar, salt, and pepper. Marinate for 1 hour in the refrigerator.

3. Divide the marinated onion among four small dishes and sprinkle each portion with a small amount of sesame seeds.

STORAGE TIP: Place in a clean container with a lid and store for up to 4 days in the refrigerator.

Savory Egg Custard (Chawanmushi)

GLUTEN-FREE,
NUT-FREE,
PESCATARIAN

Serves 4

PREP TIME:
20 minutes,
plus 1 hour
to cool

COOK TIME:
20 minutes

Chawanmushi is an amazingly delicious and soft-textured egg dish. It is a mixture of egg and dashi soup steamed together, and may include various other ingredients to taste. To cook chawanmushi, you will be placing the serving dishes in a double boiler, so the top pan will need to be higher than the serving dishes so that you can cover it with a lid.

2½ cups water

2 teaspoons Ajinomoto Hondashi bonito soup stock powder, or any dashi powder

2 teaspoons mirin

4 teaspoons soy sauce (gluten-free if necessary)

2 teaspoons cooking sake

1 teaspoon salt

4 small or medium shrimp, deveined

4 parsley sprigs, trimmed and cut into 1-inch length

2 small shiitake mushrooms, stemmed and sliced

3 eggs, beaten

1. In a saucepan, stir together the water, dashi powder, mirin, soy sauce, cooking sake, and salt. Bring the mixture to a boil over medium-high heat, and keep it boiling for 1 minute. Turn off the heat and allow the pan to cool for 1 or 2 minutes. Transfer the pan to the refrigerator for at least 1 hour, or until it gets cold.

2. Meanwhile, wrap the lid of a double boiler with paper towels or a kitchen towel. Tape or tie the towels on top of the lid, so moisture doesn't drop into the dish during cooking. Fill the bottom pan halfway with water, put the top pan on it with the lid, and bring to a boil over medium heat.

3. In a 5- to 6-ounce deep glass bowl, place a shrimp, one-quarter of the parsley, and one-quarter of the mushrooms. Prepare three more bowls with the remaining shrimp, parsley, and mushrooms.

4. Add a spoonful of the cold dashi soup to the beaten eggs, and mix well to combine and temper the eggs. Whisk the eggs gently into the dashi soup. Divide the egg mixture evenly among the prepared bowls, filling each bowl three-quarters full.

5. Place the bowls in the top pan (in batches if necessary), cover, and cook over low heat for 10 minutes. Let the bowls cool for at least 15 minutes before serving. Be careful when you eat, because the inside of the dish is very hot.

COOKING TIP: To make sure it is cooked through, the custard should be jiggly when you shake the bowl, and be sure clear soup comes out when you make a small hole with a toothpick. If not, steam for 3 more minutes. The heat should be kept low, because the egg cooks quickly and may cake on the dish and lose its soft texture with higher heat.

Tofu Salad with Sesame Dressing

GLUTEN-FREE,
NUT-FREE,
VEGAN

Serves 4

PREP TIME:
10 minutes

COOK TIME:
2 minutes

This is a very light, healthy, and delicious salad with a sesame dressing that is very popular in Japan. You can use this dressing for any kind of salad. Sesame seeds are a great source of protein, iron, niacin, and vitamin B. In addition, they have high antioxidant properties due to their vitamin E and linoleic acid. Another important ingredient in sesame seeds is lignan, which helps improve liver function and lower cholesterol.

½ (14-ounce) package firm tofu

¼ cup soy sauce (gluten-free if necessary)

¼ cup rice vinegar

2 tablespoons toasted sesame oil

2 tablespoons roasted sesame seeds

24 grape tomatoes, halved

1 cucumber, cut into ½-inch cubes

1. Drain the tofu, wrap in paper towels, and microwave for 90 seconds. Let the tofu sit for 10 minutes to drain completely. Cut into ½-inch cubes.

2. In a bowl, stir together the soy sauce, rice vinegar, sesame oil, and sesame seeds.

3. Divide the tomatoes, cucumber, and tofu among four salad dishes. Serve with the dressing on the side.

Japanese Sake
(Nihon-Shu)

Green Tea

Green tea powder is a powdered green *sencha* tea. Sencha is made from the same leaves as matcha. Sencha has a deep taste and great green tea flavor that goes well with raw and fatty sashimi and sushi, and also serves as a palate freshener. I recommend Chaganju Uji Organic Instant Sencha Green Tea Powder (80-gram bag), which is available from Amazon.

Japanese Sake (Nihon-Shu)

There are more than 10,000 sake brands in the world, so it may be difficult for people to know where to start. Japanese sake is made from a fermented mixture of rice, malted rice, and water. A sake's taste is determined by the ingredients, how much the rice is polished, and the temperature. Unlike most other brewed beverages, sake can be consumed hot, warm, at room temperature, slightly cold, and very cold.

Sake has a range of tastes and may be rich, bitter, light, fruity, or sweet. Bitter is an authentic taste for sake, and is typically the preference for many Japanese people. They will often pair it with sushi or sashimi. However, some young Japanese people are moving away from sake because of the distinctive taste. With the growing preference for beer and sweet cocktails, sparkling sakes and sake-based cocktails have become popular. If you can't find good selections of sake near you, I recommend the website Tippsy (tippsysake.com), which has numerous authentic sakes to choose from.

CHAPTER

6

Staples and Sauces

MAYONNAISE, SRIRACHA SAUCE, SWEET CHILI SAUCE, AND many more commonly used condiments have been developed into delicious sauces for sushi rolls. This chapter addresses these sauces, but it also includes familiar recipes from many sushi restaurants all over the world, traditional Japanese sauce recipes (such as ponzu and miso sesame sauce), and several recipes referenced throughout this book. These sauce recipes are very easy to cook, they are versatile for many dishes, and some of them can last for a while in the refrigerator. Be sure to use gluten-free soy sauce if you are following a gluten-free diet.

Japanese Egg Omelet

GLUTEN-FREE,
NUT-FREE,
VEGETARIAN

Makes
1 omelet or
10 pieces
for nigiri or
4 sticks for
sushi rolls

PREP TIME:
5 minutes

COOK TIME:
5 minutes

A Japanese egg omelet is basically a thick, soft, fried egg. This savory egg omelet is an original recipe I grew up with. Some other Japanese egg omelet recipes include sugar to add a slightly sweet taste. I will introduce you to two ways of making this dish. The real keys to a successful omelet is to use a non-stick pan and nonstick spray and to preheat the pan really well.

3 large eggs, beaten

2 teaspoons soy sauce
(gluten-free if necessary)

Nonstick cooking spray

TO MAKE THE TRADITIONAL VERSION

1. In a mixing bowl, stir together the eggs and soy sauce.

2. Coat a preheated nonstick rectangular skillet (5 to 6 inches by 7 inches) with cooking spray and pour one-third of the egg mixture into the skillet, being sure to spread the egg over the entire surface of the pan. Cook over medium heat for 20 seconds, until the edge of the egg is cooked and liquid is still present on top.

3. Fold the egg in three. It is okay if the egg is unshaped at this moment. Slide the egg to the far side of the pan.

4. Pour half of the remaining mixture into the empty space of the pan, lift the existing egg omelet, and let the mixture flow underneath while spreading the egg all over the surface of the pan. Cook for 30 seconds and fold into three again, then slide the egg to the far side of the pan. Repeat with the remaining egg mixture. Gently press the omelet with the spatula, and cook for 30 seconds on each side.

TO MAKE AN EASIER VERSION

1. In a mixing bowl, stir together the eggs and soy sauce.

2. Coat a preheated 8-inch nonstick skillet with cooking spray and pour all of the egg mixture into the skillet. Cook over medium-low heat for 1 minute, without stirring and until the edges of the eggs are slightly cooked.

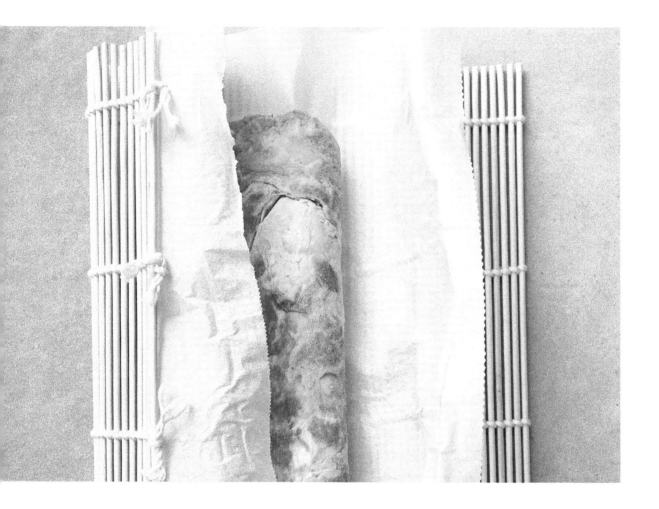

3. Using a spatula, gently gather the cooked part toward the center of the skillet and spread the uncooked egg toward the edges of the pan. Cook for 1 minute until the egg is set.

4. Fold the egg in three, gently press the omelet with the spatula, and cook for 30 seconds on each side.

5. Place the *makisu* on a work surface and cover with a piece of parchment paper or paper towel. Lay the omelet on it and wrap with the makisu to make a 1-inch-thick rectangle. Let it sit for 10 minutes at room temperature.

COOKING TIP: The omelet, wrapped in the makisu, can be stored in the refrigerator for about 2 hours to cool, so the omelet acquires a firmer shape.

Ginger Dressing

GLUTEN-FREE,
NUT-FREE,
VEGAN

Makes
1½ cups

PREP TIME:
10 minutes

This dressing is one of my favorite nontraditional Japanese recipes. When I had this at an Asian restaurant in Philadelphia for the first time, I asked the staff for the recipe because it was amazingly delicious! A food processor does all the work for you after you prepare the ingredients. To store, transfer the dressing to a glass jar and keep in the refrigerator for up to 2 weeks.

1 large carrot, coarsely chopped

½ large onion, coarsely chopped

1 (3- to 4-inch) piece fresh ginger, peeled and coarsely chopped

1 garlic clove

¼ cup soy sauce (gluten-free if necessary)

¼ cup rice vinegar

½ teaspoon salt

1 tablespoon toasted sesame oil

½ cup extra-virgin olive oil

1. In a food processor, combine the carrot, onion, ginger, garlic, soy sauce, rice vinegar, salt, sesame oil, and olive oil. Blend until somewhat smooth.

2. Transfer to a jar, cover, and keep refrigerated. Use within 2 weeks.

   COOKING TIP: The first day, the vegetables and the oil may seem barely mixed, but the dressing reaches the right consistency after a few days.

Spicy Mayonnaise Sauce

GLUTEN-FREE, NUT-FREE, VEGETARIAN

Makes about ⅓ cup

PREP TIME: 5 minutes

Needless to say, this is the most famous spicy sauce in the sushi world. Sriracha is a great sauce on its own, but when you mix it with other condiments, such as mayo, soy sauce, or miso, it can take on a whole new delicious flavor! You can use a spoon to drizzle sushi rolls with this sauce, but using a dressing bottle is better for creating impressive final presentations.

¼ cup mayonnaise

1 tablespoon sriracha sauce

1 teaspoon toasted sesame oil

In a small bowl, mix the mayonnaise, sriracha sauce, and sesame oil.

Sweet Eel Sauce

GLUTEN-FREE,
NUT-FREE,
VEGAN

Makes ½ cup

PREP TIME:
10 minutes

COOK TIME:
25 minutes

This sauce has a perfect sweet–savory taste and a thick texture. Because the sauce needs to be cooked to get the right consistency, you might want to make this sauce first in your cooking process. Or you can make this sauce ahead of time, keep in the refrigerator, and use within 1 month. If the sauce becomes very thick in the refrigerator, keep it at room temperature for at least 1 hour before you use it.

½ cup soy sauce (gluten-free if necessary)

½ cup mirin

¼ cup cooking sake

2 tablespoons sugar

1. In a saucepan, stir together the soy sauce, mirin, cooking sake, and sugar. Bring it to a boil over medium heat. Reduce the heat to low, simmer for 20 minutes, and stir occasionally until thickened. Let it cool for 10 minutes at room temperature.

2. Place the mixture in a sterilized 4-ounce dressing bottle and store in the refrigerator for up to 1 month.

Ponzu Sauce

GLUTEN-FREE,
NUT-FREE,
VEGAN

Makes ½ cup

PREP TIME:
5 minutes

Ponzu is an essential sauce in Japan and is used almost as much as soy sauce. It contains vinegar and lime juice, so it has a fresher taste than soy sauce. Japanese people use this sauce for many dishes, such as shabu-shabu, grilled fish, dim sum, fried rice, and tofu.

¼ cup soy sauce (gluten-free if necessary)

¼ cup rice vinegar

Juice of ½ lime

Combine the soy sauce, rice vinegar, and lime juice in a jar and keep in the refrigerator for up to 2 weeks.

Tempura Batter

GLUTEN-FREE,
NUT-FREE,
VEGAN

Makes about
1 cup

PREP TIME:
10 minutes

I always try to make tempura with a great crunchy (not greasy) texture because it is more delicious that way. The tempura batter recipe has a major effect on the crunchiness. Sometimes tempura batter contains egg, but I use rice vinegar instead, and it works great! The key is to use really cold water (you can even add a few ice cubes to the water before you mix) and not to overmix. That is all you need to cook delicious, crispy tempura.

½ cup cornstarch

1 teaspoon rice vinegar

1 teaspoon salt

½ cup cold water

In a small bowl, stir together the cornstarch, rice vinegar, salt, and cold water, and stir very gently until just a few lumps are left.

Tempura Dashi Sauce

GLUTEN-FREE,
NUT-FREE,
VEGAN

Makes about
1 cup

PREP TIME:
5 minutes

COOK TIME:
5 minutes

This is a light-textured, soy sauce–based sauce that has a delicious dashi flavor. Traditionally, tempura is served with this sauce or sea salt. People tend to add grated daikon radish to the sauce; the daikon works as a palate freshener for fried food. The sauce is also used as a condiment for many dishes and is a great base for soup.

1 cup water

1 teaspoon Shimaya kombu dashi soup stock powder, or any vegetable- or fish-based dashi powder

¼ cup soy sauce (gluten-free if necessary)

¼ cup mirin

1. In a saucepan, stir together the water, dashi powder, soy sauce, and mirin. Bring to a boil over medium heat. Let it cool down.

2. Transfer to an 8-ounce jar, cover, and keep in the refrigerator for up to 1 month.

Pico de Gallo

GLUTEN-FREE,
NUT-FREE,
VEGAN

Makes
2 cups

PREP TIME:
10 minutes

I was so happy when I learned this recipe. I love fresh tomato, but I didn't know many fresh tomato sauce recipes. This pico de gallo is easy, is versatile, and lasts for a week in the refrigerator. Increase or decrease jalapeño and garlic according to your preference. You might also consider using lemon instead of lime, but lime has a less sour taste than lemon and adds a touch of that special lime flavor to the dish.

2 large tomatoes, seeded and diced

10 cilantro sprigs, trimmed and minced

½ red onion, diced

2 teaspoons grated garlic

½ teaspoon salt

½ jalapeño, seeded and finely diced

Juice of 1 lime

1. In a mixing bowl, stir together the tomatoes, cilantro, onion, garlic, salt, jalapeño, and lime juice.

2. Transfer to a 16-ounce jar, cover, and keep in the refrigerator for up to 1 week.

Spicy Mango Sauce

GLUTEN-FREE,
NUT-FREE,
VEGETARIAN

Makes 1 cup

PREP TIME:
10 minutes

This mango sauce has a very fruity and a slightly spicy taste. Unlike tomato salsa, the main ingredients are mango and cilantro, so the texture is very soft. It goes really well with seafood and salads! Mango has a pit in the center like an avocado, but it is very small and sticks to the meat firmly. To remove, cut along the pit, and peel and dice with extra care because it is slippery.

1 large mango, peeled and diced

5 cilantro sprigs, trimmed and finely minced

½ teaspoon salt

Pinch freshly ground black pepper

2 teaspoons crushed red pepper

2 teaspoons rice vinegar

1 teaspoon grated garlic

2 teaspoons honey

2 teaspoons freshly squeezed lemon juice

1. In a mixing bowl, stir together the mango, cilantro, salt, black pepper, red pepper, vinegar, garlic, honey, and lemon juice.

2. Transfer to an 8-ounce jar, cover, and keep in the refrigerator for up to 1 week.

Wasabi Mayonnaise Sauce

GLUTEN-FREE,
NUT-FREE,
VEGETARIAN

Makes about
¼ cup

PREP TIME:
5 minutes

There is store-bought wasabi mayonnaise, but this recipe is easy, quick, and customizable to your taste! In this recipe, a dash of soy sauce adds a slightly salty, delicious flavor. This Japanese-style spicy mayonnaise is great for salad, grilled meat, grilled fish, and fried egg. Also, if you like yakisoba, Japanese stir-fried noodles, try adding this sauce. It is delicious!

¼ cup mayonnaise

2 teaspoons wasabi

1 teaspoon soy sauce
(gluten-free if necessary)

In a small bowl, stir together the mayonnaise, wasabi, and soy sauce.

Sweet Chili Mayonnaise Sauce

GLUTEN-FREE,
NUT-FREE,
VEGETARIAN

Makes about
¼ cup

PREP TIME:
5 minutes

This sauce has a delicious Thai flavor and an amazing combination of sweet, spicy, and sour tastes. In Japan, the sauce is commonly used for cooked shrimp dishes. Also, it is great for grilled chicken, summer rolls, and sandwiches, and as a dipping sauce for vegetables. This chili sauce has a milder taste than the Spicy Mayonnaise Sauce (page 147).

¼ cup mayonnaise   1 tablespoon sweet chili sauce

In a small bowl, stir together the mayonnaise and the chili sauce.

Soy Sauce Mayonnaise Sauce

**GLUTEN-FREE,
NUT-FREE,
VEGETARIAN**

**Makes about
⅓ cup**

PREP TIME:
5 minutes

This is a traditional Japanese seasoning mixture that I used earlier in my life to mask the taste of fish and vegetables, which I didn't like very much. This sauce is also a great marinade for fish, meat, and tofu. Sometimes mayonnaise sauces are mixed ahead of time and are transferred into jars or dressing bottles for storage. My preference, however, is to use them fresh, in order to avoid changes in texture and taste.

¼ cup mayonnaise

2 tablespoons soy sauce
(gluten-free if necessary)

In a small bowl, stir together the mayonnaise and soy sauce.

Miso Sesame Sauce

GLUTEN-FREE,
NUT-FREE,
VEGAN

Makes about
⅓ cup

PREP TIME:
5 minutes

This is a slightly sweet and highly nutritious sauce. Traditionally, this sauce is used with fried cutlets in Japan but it's also great with raw vegetables, cold tofu, and Japanese udon noodles. You can use any type of miso and sesame seeds. You can find red miso paste, white miso paste, and mixed (awase) miso in many Asian markets. Red miso paste is salty, white miso is sweet, and awase is a balance of salty and sweet.

2 tablespoons roasted
sesame seeds

2 tablespoons
miso paste

2 teaspoons toasted
sesame oil

1 tablespoon sugar

2 teaspoons water

1. In a mixing bowl, stir together the sesame seeds, miso, sesame oil, and sugar. Whisk in the water until you have a consistency you like.

2. Transfer to a 4-ounce jar and keep in the refrigerator for up to 3 weeks.

Sweet-and-Sour Sauce

GLUTEN-FREE,
NUT-FREE,
VEGAN

Makes ¼ cup

PREP TIME:
5 minutes

It may surprise you how easily you can make this delicious sauce! You can store this sauce in your refrigerator for up to 2 weeks. It's great to have on hand because it is amazing with sautéed vegetables, grilled meat, or fish. You should always use clean cutlery when serving a sauce, and it is also important to check the look and smell of any sauce before consuming.

2 tablespoons sweet
chili sauce

1 tablespoon ketchup

1 tablespoon soy sauce
(gluten-free if necessary)

1. Combine the chili sauce, ketchup, and soy sauce.

2. Transfer to a 4-ounce jar and keep in the refrigerator for up to 2 weeks.

Almond Sauce

GLUTEN-FREE,
VEGAN

Makes ¼ cup

PREP TIME:
5 minutes

This sauce has a simple, light taste, so you can use it with any kind of dish, such as salad, pasta, and sautéed dishes. Almonds are richer in nutrients and have a higher amount of vitamin E than other nuts. They are also high in minerals and fiber. This sauce can be stored for 2 weeks in the refrigerator, but be sure to stir well every time before you use the sauce.

1 tablespoon no-sugar-added and no-salt-added almond butter

Juice of ½ lemon

¼ teaspoon salt

Freshly ground black pepper

¼ teaspoon onion powder

½ teaspoon grated garlic

2 to 3 tablespoons warm water, as needed

1. In a mixing bowl, stir together the almond butter, lemon juice, salt, pepper, onion powder, and garlic. Whisk in the warm water until you have a consistency you like.

2. Transfer to a 4-ounce jar and keep in the refrigerator for up to 2 weeks.

Peanut Sauce

GLUTEN-FREE,
VEGAN

Makes ⅓ cup

PREP TIME:
5 minutes

The Asian flavors of cumin, sesame oil, ginger, and garlic make this peanut sauce amazingly delicious and complementary to sushi rolls! Peanuts have a high antioxidant effect, can help with fatigue, and are full of niacin, which means they help prevent hangovers. Make sure to use no-sugar-added and no-salt-added peanut butter because it is healthier, and it is easy to adjust the taste to your preference.

2 tablespoons no-sugar-added and no-salt-added peanut butter

1 tablespoon soy sauce (gluten-free if necessary)

1 teaspoon cumin

1 teaspoon peeled, grated fresh ginger

1 teaspoon grated garlic

1 teaspoon toasted sesame oil

1 teaspoon onion powder

Juice of ½ lemon

Salt

Freshly ground black pepper

2 to 3 tablespoons warm water, as needed

1. In a mixing bowl, stir together the peanut butter, soy sauce, cumin, ginger, garlic, sesame oil, onion powder, and lemon juice. Taste and season with salt and black pepper as needed. Whisk in the warm water until you have a consistency you like.

2. Transfer to a 4-ounce container and keep in the refrigerator for up to 2 weeks.

Pickling Liquid

GLUTEN-FREE,
NUT-FREE,
VEGAN

Makes 1 cup

PREP TIME:
5 minutes

This is a refreshing, ginger-flavored pickling liquid. This is great not only for pickling vegetables but also as a dressing and a sauce for many dishes. I love adding some pickling liquid to a rice cooker when I cook rice. Make a batch of the pickling liquid ahead of time, keep refrigerated, and use within 3 weeks. Having this liquid in your refrigerator makes your cooking process much easier!

½ cup toasted sesame oil

¼ cup soy sauce (gluten-free if necessary)

¼ cup rice vinegar

½ teaspoon salt

1 teaspoon peeled, grated fresh ginger

1. Combine the sesame oil, soy sauce, rice vinegar, salt, and ginger in an 8-ounce jar. Cover and shake to combine.

2. Store in the refrigerator for up to 3 weeks.

Tempura Batter Bits (Agedama or Tenkasu)

Makes ¼ cup

PREP TIME:
5 minutes

COOK TIME:
15 minutes

Tempura batter bits are often used as a garnish for side dishes because the bits actually have a hearty flavor from the tempura ingredients. The best tips to cook great agedama are to use a nonstick skillet and to move a small spoon in a circular motion over the skillet when you drop the batter in, so the small drops of the batter are splashed evenly in the oil.

2 tablespoons cornstarch

2 tablespoons water

½ teaspoon salt

Vegetable oil, for frying

1. In a small bowl, stir together the cornstarch, water, and salt.

2. In a nonstick skillet, heat ½ inch of vegetable oil over medium-low heat until it shimmers. Using a small spoon, put small drops of the mixture in the oil until the dots of the mixture almost cover the bottom of the pan. Fry for 4 to 5 minutes, stirring occasionally, until it browns slightly. Using a mesh skimmer, transfer the bits to a plate lined with paper towels to drain. Repeat with the remaining mixture.

3. When it cools down, transfer to a freezer bag and store in the freezer for up to 1 month. Use without thawing.

Pickled Sushi Ginger (Gari)

GLUTEN-FREE,
NUT-FREE,
VEGAN

Makes about
½ cup

PREP TIME:
10 minutes,
plus 12 hours
to marinate

COOK TIME:
2 minutes

Sushi ginger recipes call for young ginger, which is also called spring ginger. Young ginger tastes mild (you can even eat it raw), and has a juicy, soft, smooth texture with a pink blush. If you use regular ginger, not young ginger, slice very thinly and soak in water for at least 12 to 24 hours before starting to prepare this recipe. Even if the ginger is prepared properly, the taste may still be spicy, and the texture may still be tough and fibrous.

2 ounces young ginger

½ cup rice vinegar

3 tablespoons sugar

1 teaspoon salt

1. Peel the ginger with a small spoon if it has a thick skin. Slice very thinly with a slicer or peeler.

2. Fill a saucepan with water. Bring the water to a boil over high heat, add the ginger, and cook for 2 minutes. Drain and let it cool.

3. Combine the vinegar, sugar, and salt and microwave for 20 seconds to melt the sugar. Mix well.

4. Wring out the ginger by hand and add the ginger and the sauce to a 4-ounce jar. Marinate in the refrigerator for at least 12 hours.

Planning Your Sushi Feast

At a sushi party, hand-rolled (*temaki*) sushi is the best for entertaining. It is easy for the hosts to prepare, and guests can enjoy "build-your-own" sushi.

How to Prepare Temaki Sushi for a Party

1. Cook 1 cup of Sushi Rice (page 17) per person. Place the rice in a big bowl along with a rice paddle, and cover with a damp kitchen towel and keep at room temperature until ready to use.

2. Prepare vegetables and cooked fillings.

   - Line a serving plate with some torn lettuce leaves and put each filling on a piece of lettuce.

   - Provide chopsticks or small tongs along with the serving plate.

   - Fried food, such as fried chicken and shrimp tempura, can be made ahead of time and frozen for up to 1 month. On the day of the party, you can reheat for 10 to 20 minutes, depending on the quantity, in a 400°F oven.

   - It is better to prepare approximately three times the number of pieces of each ingredient as the number of people who will attend.

3. Prepare refrigerated fillings.

   - It is preferable to use separate dishes for fish and shellfish.

   - Keep refrigerated until right before serving.

   - Prepare approximately two to three times the number of pieces of each ingredient as the number of people who will attend.

4. Prepare wraps: Serve nori, lettuce, and thin fried egg as wrappers on a plate.

   ◆ Use a whole nori sheet per person and cut into quarters, so each piece of nori is approximately square shaped.

   ◆ Wash and dry lettuce leaves, and tear them to about the same size as the cut nori.

   ◆ Using one egg per guest, cook the thin fried eggs (see steps 1 and 2 of Egg and Salmon Roe Temari, page 54).

5. Prepare sauces: Use dressing or squeeze bottles for each homemade sauce, such as Spicy Mayonnaise Sauce (page 147), Sweet Eel Sauce (page 148), and/or Miso Sesame Sauce (page 157). It is good to have plain mayonnaise, as well.

Resources

CATALINA OFFSHORE PRODUCTS: has high-quality fish, a big selection, and great reviews. It is located in San Diego. www.store.catalinaop.com

DINING WITH THE CHEF: JAPANESE FOOD: a great resource for Japanese recipes. www.nhk.or.jp/dwc/food

GREAT BRITISH CHEFS: the team behind the fastest-growing food websites in the UK. www.greatbritishchefs.com

JAPANESE CHEFS KNIFE: established in 2003, a division of the Kencrest Corporation, they sell knives direct to consumers. www.japanesechefsknife.com

JAPANNY: dedicated to promoting the traditional and high-end handmade Japanese kitchen knives. www.japanny.com

NOAA FISHERIES: provides information on sustainable seafood. www.fisheries.noaa.gov/insight/understanding-sustainable-seafood

OCEANSIDE SEAFOOD: has been serving Michigan since 1980 with great seafood products. It has good shipping deals for those of you located in the northeastern Midwest. www.oceansideseafood.com

SIROGOHAN-白ごはん.COM: a great compilation of sushi recipes, in Japanese only. www.sirogohan.com

TIPPSY SAKE: online retailer of sake. www.tippsysake.com

Recipe Label Index

Index

Acknowledgments

A special thank-you to my mother, who passed away when I was 20 years old. I appreciate that she always taught me many things and led me in the direction that is best for me. She is the inspiration that drove me to write my blog and this book, and she is the source of many of the recipes here. I wish she could read this book. I miss you so much, Mom.

Thank you to my husband, Frank, for your endless love and support even though you are super busy as a law professor. You always reassured me while I was writing this book, because you have so much experience with publishers and with writing books. Moreover, I really appreciate your many funny jokes that always calm me down when I am stressed out.

Thank you to my grandmother, who is 95 years old and still lives by herself. She taught me how to cut up a whole fish, which my grandfather caught each day when I was little. Her favorite phrase is "If the dish is bland, add seasoning. If the dish has too strong taste, cook with more water. That's it!" She inspired me to recognize that cooking need not be difficult at all.

About the Author

CHIKA RAVITCH is the author of *Bento for Beginners*. She is a certificated facial masseuse and a makeup artist in Japan. She has a degree in analytical chemistry and wrote her senior thesis on the effects of lithium on the human body and mental health. From there, she worked for a Japanese cosmetics company, VECUA, for several years. She was an area manager, which made her responsible for overseeing five shops throughout the Kansai region. In this role she was able to learn a lot about business management and about the benefits of Japanese approaches to healthy living.

As an executive at VECUA, she was able to get special training every month on things such as nutrition, skin biology, the effect of cosmetic ingredients on the skin, and human biology. When she moved to the United States, she immediately noticed the prevalence of unhealthy and processed food. She decided to use her knowledge to teach people who want to learn about Japanese nutrition and cooking how to make traditional homemade Japanese dishes that are healthy and delicious. That is why she started the blog Japanese-food.org.

CPSIA information can be obtained
at www.ICGtesting.com
Printed in the USA
JSHW031423021121
19890JS00004B/5